A CONSULTANCY APPROACH FOR TRAINERS

A Consultancy Approach for Trainers

**Keri Phillips and
Patricia Shaw**

Gower

© Keri Phillips, Patricia Shaw 1989

Published by
Gower Publishing Company Limited
Gower House
Croft Road
Aldershot
Hants GU11 3HR
England

British Library Cataloguing in Publication Data

Phillips, Keri
   A consultancy approach for trainers.
   1. Management consultancy
   I. Title   II. Shaw, Patrica
   658.4'6

ISBN 0 566 02737 2

Printed in Great Britain by
Billing & Sons Ltd, Worcester

Contents

Preface

In recent years we have worked closely with many training and development staff, helping them make the transition into consultancy. Some have been individuals attending the Brunel Management Programme, who were either moving towards internal consulting roles or contemplating becoming independent consultants. Others have been members of the training teams within organizations to whom we have acted as consultants. As a result we have gained insight into the nature of this transition in a number of diverse organizations and with people whose backgrounds have varied considerably.

It soon became apparent to us that when our clients talked about moving from training to consulting they could mean very different things. Our need to clarify the real objectives of some of our consulting assignments led us to develop the framework on which this book is based.

We present both theoretical ideas and some practical illustrations of consultancy in action. We are writing primarily for those whose purpose as consultants is to enable client learning and development *and* whose background is in training. Trainers have experience, knowledge and skills which can be a springboard for developing as effective consultants but which can also be a hindrance. We hope our map of the territory will be useful for those making the transition themselves and for those, such as training managers, who are responsible for supporting the development of others. Our aim has been to write not a self-

contained guide but a book which excites curiosity and a desire
for further exploration.

There are many whose contribution to this book we would like
to acknowledge: heads of T and D functions who consented to be
interviewed; participants on workshops who provided ideas and
tested our thinking; friends and colleagues who have offered
encouragement and challenge; other consultants on whose
experience we have drawn; clients who have collaborated with us
on assignments; and individuals who have been influential in our
own development as consultants.

It is with such people in mind that we are grateful to: Gavin
Houston (who also provided many helpful comments on the
draft text), John Adams, Sabina Spencer, Petrūska Clarkson,
Maria Gilbert, Malcolm Reynolds, Tony Crompton, Andy
Logan, Graham Stickland, Peter Phillipson, Margaret Neale,
Phil Merry, John Wornell, Jackie Draper, and the members of
Partners for Development – Graham Pratt, Jeanette Taylor,
Nancy Paul and David Tyrell. We would particularly like to
thank our colleague, Paul Roberts, for his continuing support
and inspiration and Yvonne Shaw for her indefatigable help in
typing and retyping the manuscript.

Keri Phillips
Patricia Shaw

1 Change and the Trainer

This chapter offers an overview of the trends which are leading increasing numbers of trainers to become consultants, both within organizations and as independent professionals. Its aim is to help trainers broaden their understanding of the context in which this change in role is taking place. This is important for those who are committed to the change for the sake of their own personal and professional development, and who still need to convince others in the organization of the validity and relevance of their aspirations. We are also writing for those who may be struggling to come to terms with new and perhaps unwelcome demands being imposed upon them.

We start by outlining some of the changes taking place in organizations and the implications for managerial effectiveness. We then look at how the role of the trainer has evolved over the last 30 years. Finally we suggest how the role of consultant fits the management and organizational development needs of many of today's companies.

Organizational changes

It has become a truism to say that we live in times of rapid and increasing change. The references at the end of this chapter are just a sample of the large numbers of books that discuss the impact of social, economic and technological change on organizations.[1,2,3,4]

Some of the main themes are:

Economic change: emergence of the global economy; the inter-dependence of markets and finance in which the simple rules of free market enterprise no longer apply.

Technological change: enormous strides in our ability to store, access, manipulate and communicate information of all kinds at great speed.

Social change: a more varied workforce (no longer only the male breadwinner), more education but less traditional employment; a re-examination of the role of work and a greater consciousness of health and environmental issues.

The words which seem to describe our present and future world are complexity, interdependence and change, to which organiztion have reacted in various ways. Some have responded to the changed economic pressures by slimming down and exercising tighter control over all functions, whereas others have decentralized and set up highly autonomous divisions. Microprocessing is eroding whole layers of middle management and organizations are experimenting with new, more flexible organizational structures. Companies are reflecting new needs and new values in society by, for example, introducing more flexible work patterns, funding health screening for all employees, implementing equal opportunity policies and taking greater social responsibility.

Some of the most interesting developments are taking place where organizations are grappling not just with the impact of *each* change but with the fact of *continuous* change itself. Much of the received wisdom about the successful management of organizations assumed a relatively stable environment in which many of our large bureaucratic organizations flourished. The acceptance of rapid change as the context has seen a new emphasis on flexibility and creativity – as in the emerging popularity of the following.

Being 'close to the customer'

'Customer Care'[5] programmes, such as those mounted by British Airways, British Rail and Lloyds Bank, are intended to educate the whole workforce towards a greater awareness and responsiveness to changing customer needs. A less visible example of the same trend is the attempt by some parts of the computer industry to involve customers in the design of new products, a step which goes beyond traditional market research by bringing the customer into the activities of the company.

Entrepreneurship

The fostering of individual initiative in order to harness creativity within the organization[6] has progressed beyond the suggestion box to quality circles on the shop floor, where employees are actively involved in seeking out ways to improve productivity. In organizations where new products are vital for maintaining a competitive edge, such as in 3M and Hewlett-Packard,[7] individuals with bright ideas are funded to escape from and sometimes fight against the system as if they were a totally autonomous business unit. Rank Xerox go further, helping sections of their workforce to leave the parent organization and set up small businesses which sell back services or goods to their former employer.[8]

Multi-disciplinary structures

Traditional hierarchical structures are not adequate for coping with rapid change. Looked at simply an organization cannot respond quickly to changes in customer requirements if approval is needed from many different layers of authority and across rigidly separated functions. More organizations are making use of matrix management and cellular structures that encourage multiple links across divisions. Multi-disciplinary teams to see through particular projects are formed. Here ability and expertise are more important than hierarchical position.

Networking

Networking may refer to both technology and people. Information is now a primary resource and desk top terminals allow rapid exchange of data and ideas between all levels within a company and access to information from sources all over the world. Digital Equipment Co. promote creative problem-solving by enabling their engineers to type in questions to their terminal and receive help and suggestions from their colleagues. This idea of peer self-help and mutual development can be seen equally in the spread of support groups and action learning sets.[9] Here small groups of managers meet regularly to exchange ideas and pool experience in order to implement projects or find concrete solutions to management problems.

Corporate Statements of purpose

The challenge for many organizations is to balance, on the one hand, greater flexibility and diversity, and fewer structural blocks to individual initiative, with, on the other hand, a strong sense of corporate identity and direction. In consequence, companies have been formulating 'mission statements' and 'codes of values' which are intended to inspire and align employees to a shared central purpose or vision.[10] Such statements often include 'hard' targets (e.g. 25 per cent of sales should be from products less than 5 years old) and 'soft' values (e.g. to respect the dignity and worth of individuals).

The consequences of change for managers

Change in organizations implies change in the way people manage and the skills and qualities required of them. The consequence seems to be an increase in the sheer range of competences being expected of managers.

We have asked several groups of senior (mostly male) managers attending programmes on organizational change to list the personal skills and qualities they believe are now needed for effectiveness. The following list is typical:

Flexibility and creativity
Entrepreneurial skills
Vision
Natural authority
Diagnostic skills
Problem-solving skills
Leadership

Risk-taking
Accurate judgement
Ability to use *all* available skills and contributions
Teamwork
Consulting skills
Decision-making skills
Self-development and self-awareness
Coaching and counselling skills
Ability to think strategically
Ability to see the 'big picture'
Interpersonal skills
Sensitivity
Ability to motivate
A high pain threshold!

It is a diverse list that points to management as an increasingly demanding occupation. We have selected five priorities.

The ability to handle complexity and ambiguity

Managers need to be able to create and recreate the systems they work in and to define their own roles and tasks. To achieve this without undue stress takes what Edgar Schein has called emotional competence – the capacity to be stimulated rather than exhausted by the rate of change and to be able to bear high levels of self-responsibility without becoming paralysed.[11]

The ability to draw on the less traditional sources of power

As organizational structures flatten and cross-functional links are formed, managers can rely less on position or rank for their authority. Similarly the specialist cannot expect the depth of his or her expertise to guarantee influence. High levels of personal and consulting skills are needed.

Leadership abilities

Managing greater diversity and flexibility requires leadership which is not characterized by control but by the capacity to give direction, define outcomes and inspire individual effort towards common goals. There is also increasing attention being paid to organizational cultures and the role of the manager as a creator and carrier of that culture,[12] which demands a heightened awareness of how behavioural norms are created, maintained and changed.

The ability to develop self and others

With greater emphasis on the importance of people, managers need to understand how adults learn and be skilful in coaching, counselling and developing staff. The accent is on self-development. The only efficient way in which companies can ensure all employees learn faster than the rate of change is to make each person actively responsible for his or her own development. For example Bob Garratt has written about the need for 'learning organizations'[13] and for managers to become less reliant on past experience, less influenced by other managers' methods and less compelled towards instant activity.

The ability to work effectively in teams and groups

When interdependence is vital, managers need to be able to understand and use group dynamics to form, build and dissolve teams quickly and to move smoothly between leadership and membership roles. They also need to recognize and value individual differences and to be able to work with a variety of styles and preferences. Businesses that need quick responses to changing conditions cannot afford the sleepy pace and demotivation of stagnant committees and badly run meetings.

As a way of summarizing what we have said so far, we shall use a model originally developed by two of our colleagues, John Adams and Sabina Spencer.[14] It is based on two dimensions. That of time scale is self-explanatory. The other is centred on attention, i.e. the extent to which managers in organizations generally focus *outwards* towards external problems and constraints or look *inward* for direction, using intuition and insight. When these areas are combined, they form four basic orientations to organizational life: operate, innovate, anticipate and create. See Figure 1.1.

OUTER SHORT ——————— TIMESCALE ——————— LONG	
OPERATE Deals with immediate problems; corrects deviations; focuses on short-term results; maintains consistency; uses available resources.	**ANTICIPATE** Finds out about and plans to meet future needs, problems and expectations; keeps abreast of trends within and outside the organization.
INNOVATE Improves existing methods and products; uses current skills and knowledge in new ways; tolerates mistakes.	**CREATE** Encourages learning, exploration and creativity directed towards a unifying purpose and vision; designs the future.

(left margin reads vertically: A T T E N T I O N between OUTER and INNER)

Figure 1.1   Timescale/attention model

Traditionally organizations have put resources into the 'operate' and 'anticipate' quadrants. Formalized procedures and strategic planning were both efficient and effective in a relatively stable environment, but this largely analytical approach is found wanting as the rate of change accelerates. Hence the shift towards the 'innovate' and 'create' quadrants.[15]

The implications of change for trainers

The last decade has been a difficult one for traditional training and development functions. They were amongst the first casualties of cutbacks in the 1970s as organizations looked for what seemed the easiest places to reduce numbers and budgets. Redundancies were rife, Industrial Training Boards were run down, company training centres were sold, morale suffered. Yet the late 1980s are seeing the emergence of a revitalized profession, born of new business imperatives.

When the strategic resource was capital, organizations treated people as a vital, but nevertheless rather uniform resource. With high premiums now being placed on innovation, creativity, vision and communication, a company's employees really are the key to success. As organizations make greater demands of people and the necessary levels of knowledge and skill become more scarce, the development of staff becomes increasingly central to the business needs of companies. The buoyancy of the profession can be witnessed in the way the number of independent consul-tants is multiplying; in the success of management consultancies attached to the large accountancy firms moving into the field of human resource development; and in the expansion of demand for the services of management training colleges and business schools.

Those internal training and development functions which survived the bleak times have changed or are changing; just as organizations are paying closer attention to their external environment, so training and development functions are listen-ing even more closely to their customers. What they are hearing is likely to include some or all of the following:

- We want less delay between the identification and the meet-ing of development needs.
- We want development which is tailored to our different requirements rather than training courses which attempt to satisfy generalized needs.
- We want more development to take place with complete work groups and teams.
- We want more flexibility and variety in the nature of develop-ment activities.
- We want development activities which, in themselves, contri-bute to business results.
- We want to be able to assess more clearly the outcomes and benefits of development activities.

As training and development functions struggle to find ways of meeting these demands, we have noticed the following trends in both the public and private sector.

Less set menu, more à la carte

Short modules are replacing lengthy programmes. There are far fewer 2- or 3-week middle management programmes, for exam-ple. Instead there are more 2- or 3-day courses on very specific areas, and more 1-day workshops, short seminars, management briefings, training updates, team-building events.

More active marketing of services

Even in the Civil Service, budgeting authority is being devolved. Managers have more say in how they spend their budgets, e.g. whether to use internal or external resources. At the same time there has been a move towards training and development departments becoming profit centres, charging for their services and competing directly with external consultancies. A marketing mentality is leading T & D functions to find out more about the needs of potential users and to involve them more in designing development strategies. It also means that more attention is being paid to educating managers to make the best use of the function's resources.

An increase in self-development approaches

Recognizing the diversity of development needs is leading to more self-directed learning activities on courses, more use of open and distance learning methods and computer-based packages, more action-learning sets and self-development groups. Support networks are encouraged to carry course learning back into the work environment. Project work is designed to do the same and there are moves to increase pre-course work by participants in order to release trainers from their didactic role on programmes. Even the use of course handouts is diminishing as participants generate their own material.

A move out of the training room

A classroom, however informal the layout, is no longer the main or only setting in which trainers work. They are to be found out and about, in managers' offices, in the boardroom, on the shop floor, using the outdoors. Even their traditional props – wallcharts, flipcharts, whiteboards, video and audio equipment – are to be found in use throughout the organization.

Just as the roles of managers have changed, becoming more varied and demanding, so the role of the trainer has expanded over the last 30 years.[16,17] When training meant fitting individuals for pre-determined job requirements, the trainer as an instructor or lecturer was perfectly adequate. When the knowledge and skills needed to perform a certain job were seen as clear-cut and consistent over time, then employees could be sent on standard courses. Training was a low-status, marginalized activity.

The impact of the behavioural sciences and humanistic values on management theory and practice in the 1950s and 1960s meant that trainers started to pay more attention to the personal development of employees. Staff and management trainers were accorded higher status than technical trainers and were expected to become more participative in their approach. Human relations and interpersonal skills training came to the fore, but trainers were still able to operate effectively in 'training laboratories' and training centres away from the mainstream of organizational life. Indeed this isolation from the normal working environment was seen as an essential condition for this type of training.

During the 1970s, when the recession started to bite, training of this sort went out of favour, and there was a return to training that could be more obviously related to the 'bottom line'. Trainers became problem-solvers in areas where lack of knowledge, poor preparation for promotion, inadequate adjustment to new organizational structures or unsatisfactory performance were hampering organizational effectiveness. Trainers needed to work more closely with managers to identify needs and to design or organize suitable courses. Trainers became part of a service function to line management along with personnel, corporate planning and computer services. By the end of the decade they were part trainer, part administrator and part internal consultant.

The shift of emphasis from training to learning has redefined the trainer's specialism. In 1985 Eugene Donnelly described a trainer as a 'manager of learning'.[18] A few years earlier the University of Lancaster introduced its MA in Management Learning, designed especially for training and development professionals.

At the time of writing the changes we have outlined are still shaping the new role. Enabling others to lead and manage continuous change, with all the consequences we have described, involves the trainer as a facilitator of organizational change and development. The word trainer is becoming increasingly inadequate for describing this role. Practitioners are struggling to find new labels. Charles Margerison, for example, writes of the 'active educational architect'.[19]

In a relatively short period, then, the role of the trainer has evolved dramatically into one with far greater scope and potential influence. The implications are many: for the career development of trainers whose skills and experience were gained in very different times, for the recruitment of people capable of creating and developing new roles, for the management of a function whose staff may span the range from instructor to consultant, for finding the right balance in using internal and external resources. In the following chapters we set out what we have learned about ways in which these implications can be successfully handled.

Notes

1. Robertson, J. *FUTURE WORK*, Temple Smith/Gower 1985.
2. Handy, C. *THE FUTURE OF WORK*, Blackwell 1985.
3. Naisbitt, J. and Aburdene, P. *REINVENTING THE CORPORATION*, Macdonald 1985.
4. Toffler, A. *THE ADAPTIVE CORPORATION*, Pan/Gower 1985.
5. Peters, T.J. and Waterman, R.H. *IN SEARCH OF EXCELLENCE*, Harper and Row 1982.
6. Kanter, R.M. *THE CHANGE MASTERS*, Counterpoint 1985.
7. Pinchot III, G. 'How Intrapreneurs Innovate', *MANAGEMENT TODAY*, December 1985.
8. Judkins, P., Weston, D. and Drew, J. *NETWORKING IN ORGANIZA-TIONS – THE RANK XEROX EXPERIMENT*, Gower 1985.
9. Revans, R. *ACTION LEARNING: NEW TECHNIQUES FOR MAN-AGEMENT*, Blond and Briggs, 1980.
10. Adams, J.D. (ed.) *TRANSFORMING WORK*, Miles River Press 1984.
11. Schein, E.H. CAREER DYNAMICS: MATCHING INDIVIDUAL AND ORGANIZATIONAL NEEDS, Addison-Wesley 1978.
12. Schein, E.H. *ORGANIZATIONAL CULTURE AND LEADERSHIP*, Jossey-Bass 1986.
13. Garratt, R. *THE LEARNING ORGANIZATION: THE NEED FOR DIRECTORS WHO THINK*, Fontana/Gower 1987.
14. Adams, J. and Spencer, S. 'Why Strategic Planning Fails', *STRATEGIC DIRECTIONS*, October 1986.
15. Hurst, D.K. 'Of Boxes, Bubbles and Effective Management', *HARVARD BUSINESS REVIEW*, May–June 1984.
16. Davies, J. 'Patterns and Paradoxes of Trainers' Careers: the implications for the influence of training.' *JOURNAL OF EUROPEAN INDUS-TRIAL TRAINING* Vol. 9. No. 5, 1985.

17. Pettigrew, A.H., Jones G. and Reason, P.W. *ORGANIZATIONAL AND BEHAVIOURAL ASPECTS OF THE ROLE OF THE TRAINING OFFICER IN THE U.K. CHEMICAL INDUSTRY: A RESEARCH STUDY IN TWO PHASES IN THE CHEMICAL INDUSTRY*, Chemical and Allied Products Industry Training Board 1981.
18. Donnelly, E. 'Tomorrow's Industrial Training Officer the challenge of change', *JOURNAL OF EUROPEAN INDUSTRIAL TRAINING*, Vol. 9. No. 5, 1985.
19. Margerison, C. 'Developing Managers', in Bennett, R. (ed.). *IMPROVING TRAINER EFFECTIVENESS*, Gower 1987.

2 Three Development Paths for Trainers

When the label 'trainer' is given to people working in very different ways, it quickly becomes confusing to talk about the changing role of trainers. Job titles are being coined all the time; some of them are new and some of them are already in use in other fields. Rarely do these terms have shared meanings. These are just some of the phrases we have come across recently:

Development consultant
Learning specialist
Educational architect
Manager of learning

The cynic might well raise an eyebrow at this rash of new labels, but to us their appearance is symptomatic of a struggle to redefine ways in which someone in the field of management development can work. Such redefinition seems inevitable when a role is evolving, but for the sake of clarity in this book we need to pin down the meaning of the terms we choose to use. We start by distinguishing between four ways of working, attaching a label to each one:

Trainer
Training consultant
Learning consultant
Organization change consultant

13

Examining the differences between these enables us to identify three broad developmental paths for trainers:

(a) from training to consulting,
(b) from training to learning,
(c) from individual change to organizational change.

The rest of this chapter explores these ideas in detail.

Trainer

A trainer is involved primarily in face-to-face work with groups of people on courses, seminars or workshops. The trainer uses a range of methods for giving individuals the opportunity to acquire knowledge and skills for increasing their effectiveness back at work (lectures, discussions, exercises, role-plays, case studies and simulations).

The trainer often designs and runs programmes to meet a range of *job-related needs* in the organization. Examples would be induction training for new entrants, training for first-line supervisors, equal opportunity training for all employees, interviewing skills training for managers involved in recruitment, consulting and influencing skills training for internal advisers and training in finance for non-financial managers.

Trainers may also design and run courses to meet a range of training needs which have been identified as important aspects of staff competence, whatever their specific jobs. These might include training in communication skills, assertiveness, team membership and leadership skills, creative problem solving, presentation skills and time management.

Trainers are responsible to the training department for providing a service to the rest of the organization which contributes to its overall effectiveness. Trainers may also spend time in various administrative, supervisory and other activities associated with running a series of training courses.

Training consultant

He or she mounts a single training programme or series of training programmes tailored to meet the training needs of a particular group in the organization. Although still responsible to the training department for providing a service, the training consultant works with a sponsoring client for each project. The consultant's role is to help the client use training to deal with problems related to staff effectiveness in the area for which the client is responsible.

Whereas for the trainer the training programme is the culmination and main focus of work, for the training consultant the training programme is part of the implementation stage of a consulting project. Examples might include training in team leadership skills for the project team leaders reporting to the computer services manager; the conduct of effective meetings for the trade union official and personnel manager; and assertiveness skills for administrative staff reporting to the customer services manager at a local office.

Sometimes the sponsoring client may invite the services of the training consultant, sometimes the consultant may take the initiative in persuading a potential client he or she could help in increasing the effectiveness of the client's team, section or department. Training consultants may run the training programmes themselves or organize other internal or external resources to do this.

Learning consultant

The learning consultant also works with a sponsoring client to increase the effectiveness of that part of the organization for which the client is responsible. However, the *training consultant* designs a *linear* process whereby:

1. Problems are analysed in terms of individual and group training needs.
2. These people then attend a training programme designed to give them the opportunity to acquire the specific knowledge and skills identified.
3. These people transfer the learning to their work activities.

The *learning consultant* designs a *simultaneous* process whereby:

1. Problems are analysed in terms of individual and group development needs.

2. These people engage in activities designed to enable them to learn *through* their work.

Although this may mean that groups still attend a development programme, the learning consultant works with live issues and tasks, whereas the training consultant works mainly with simulated material.

The objective of the learning consultant is to facilitate the self and mutual development of staff in a way that is integrated into work activities. Examples could include using a monthly project team meeting for a team-building event, helping a marketing group learn creative problem-solving techniques as they work on difficulties associated with promoting a new product, being a set adviser to an action learning group of managers, acting as a third party at an appraisal interview where both manager and subordinate are learning about feedback and joint goal-setting skills.

As with the training consultant, any development activity or event designed and facilitated by the learning consultant will be part of the implementation stage of a consulting project with a sponsoring client.

Organization change consultant

His or her work is similar to that of the learning consultant but with a different focus. Where the latter facilitates *individual* change and development in order to increase organizational effectiveness, the organization change consultant facilitates the change and development of the *whole organization*. In practice this means that the organization change consultant works as though the whole organization is the client, whichever individual manager or group she or he is collaborating with on a particular project.

In this sense the work starts to merge with that of the traditional organizational development (OD)[1] consultant, but instead of a background in designing large systems change, the organization change consultant works, like the learning consultant, from a thorough understanding of the learning process.

The organization change consultant builds an extra layer into the design of development activities by *explicitly* addressing how the activity contributes to the direction of desired change in the organization. Clearly in order to be able to do this the consultant needs to be working with those who are formulating the long-term strategy and medium-term goals for the company. He or she then works with sponsoring clients to enable them to learn how to be more effective in setting and meeting departmental, section, team and individual objectives in this context.

The task of the organizational change consultant is to support change by creating a learning organization where active participation in the design of change is encouraged at all levels, and where individuals learn and develop through this process. Examples could include facilitating senior management planning meetings; acting as an adviser to working parties; mediating between departments, sections, and layers of management; facilitating visioning and change workshops; and reviewing the implementation of change strategies with line managers.

Figure 2.1 summarizes and compares these four ways of working.

By way of illustration, we now introduce four case studies.

Case 1: Training

A large government department had conducted a survey of training needs amongst executive officer grades which revealed a concern about a lack of assertion and influencing skills. Although these areas formed a part of general supervisory and management training courses, the training department wanted to offer a short module specifically to address these aspects of personal effectiveness. The trainers involved in the project reviewed the training needs data and designed a workshop which would stand alone but fit into the menu of training programmes offered by the training department.

Trainees were introduced to the concept of personal power and a model of the attitudes, feelings and behaviours which support it. They engaged in a number of exercises to explore these ideas and assessed themselves against this framework.

They then undertook role-play work centred on work issues of concern to them, in order to practise the new skills and ease the application of learning back at work.

	TRAINER	TRAINING CONSULTANT	LEARNING CONSULTANT	ORGANIZATION CHANGE CONSULTANT
PRIMARY CONTRACT	With trainee on training programme	With client sponsor	With client sponsor	With whole organization through client sponsor
FOCUS OF WORK	Running training programmes	Providing tailored training	Facilitating self and mutual development	Facilitating organizational change and development
DIAGNOSIS IN TERMS OF	General organizational training needs	Client's management problem and associated training needs	Blocks to effectiveness in client's area of responsibility and associated development needs	Blocks to desired direction of organizational change in client's area of responsibility and associated development needs
IMPACT ON ORGANIZATIONAL EFFECTIVENESS	Diffused	Localized	Localized	Focused
MATERIAL WORKED WITH	Mainly simulated	Simulated and live	Mainly live	Live
APPLICATION	Requires transfer of learning to work situation and work relationships	Requires transfer of learning to work situation	Learning and working are simultaneous	Learning and working are simultaneous

Figure 2.1 Four approaches to training and consultancy

Case 2: Training consultancy

A director of a private health insurance company was responsible for negotiating an employee health screening contract with
a large customer organization. As well as administering a
number of agreed tests, screening staff were expected to offer
health education counselling to the company's employees.
Although the screening staff had basic counselling skills, the
client wanted to mount a specific training programme for the
staff involved on the project.

The training consultants helped him to draw up the performance criteria for these staff and interviewed them to find out
what difficulties they were encountering in their early work on
the project. They designed a training programme in collaboration with their client, where he covered essential medical knowledge and they covered associated counselling skills and concepts. All course materials, case studies and exercises were
tailored to match actual experiences with the project. The training consultants arranged to visit the staff on site some time after
the training course to help with any difficulties encountered in
applying the course learning, to feedback to them data collected
on the impact of the screening project to date and to assess the
need for further training.

Case 3: Learning consultancy

A large multi-national organization had moved from a structure
whereby each country was responsible for the marketing and
distribution of the whole product range within national boundaries to one in which cross-European product groups were
responsible for different product ranges. There was concern
within European headquarters that these groups were struggling
with a number of blocks to their effectiveness, including communication problems, cross-cultural differences and conflicting
interests between the European group and individual member
countries. The role of the learning consultants was to work with
the leaders of a number of these management teams to design
development which would enable task achievement and learning
to take place simultaneously.

The teams held regular 2-day meetings and in each case one of these was extended to allow time for team development. The effectiveness of the group was added as an agenda item and the consultants were facilitators during the meeting. Before attending, the managers completed an inventory, the data from which was then used at the meeting to explore the individual differences of style and temperament each brought to the group. This led to exchanges of feedback, wants and offers which would enable each person to be most effective in this setting. As the meeting progressed, the group was encouraged to monitor how well they were implementing their agreements with each other. They broke into smaller groups to address priority areas of concern and reported back to the meeting with suggestions for improvement. They reviewed the entire meeting to extract learning about group development, effective problem-solving and decision-making. All the material generated during the meeting was typed and circulated to all members. A regular review of progress was added as an agenda item for future meetings.

Case 4: Organization change consultancy

A large firm of economic planning and computer consultants had recently combined a number of divisions to form a management consulting group. The directors of this group had some clear goals for the future but strategy was still being formulated. Discussions between the organization change consultants and some of the directors revealed a number of blocks to the direction of desired change. These included:

1. An expert approach to consultancy which was the hallmark of the traditional background of the firm.
2. Sharp divisions between the disciplines within the group. Little sense of unity of purpose and standards within the new group.
3. Some disaffection amongst consultants about their own lack of development within the firm.

The aim of the assignment was to help the group develop a unified approach to consulting, improve multi-disciplinary teamwork and develop individual skills.

The consultants designed an approach whereby a selected group of staff who were seen as capable of influencing the future of the group attended a development programme. They were given reading about consulting styles, and staff from each discipline talked to the others about their work in this context. The implications for collaborative work between disciplines and with clients was explored, in terms of the stages of consultancy and in relation to current projects. Once the group had grasped the nature of the change in style, they applied the ideas to change within their own organization. They reviewed the future goals document which the managing director had talked through with them and they worked together to diagnose the blocks to change within the company.

The consultants then acted as third parties to a meeting between the staff and the directors where the staff experimented with establishing a collaborative relationship with the directors for influencing and shaping strategies for the future. This then led to a number of cross-disciplinary teams being set up to progress priority areas such as marketing the management consultancy and drawing up a code of values and working practices for the group.

These examples are intended to give a flavour of four ways of meeting the training and development needs of organizations, as we outlined them in Chapter 1. The order in which we have described them reflects a possible sequence of development for trainers. The move from trainer to training consultant to learning consultant to organization change consultant is a move along the following dimensions:

Narrower	ORGANIZATIONAL PERSPECTIVE	Wider
Lesser	DEGREE OF INFLUENCE	Greater
Shorter	TIMESCALE OF PROJECTS	Longer
Single	LEVELS OF WORKING	Multiple
Reactive	ORIENTATION	Proactive

However, to suggest this is the main or only way trainers can develop would be simplistic. There will be different starting points and different goals for different individuals. For this reason, instead of writing about sequential development we have found it more useful to describe three parallel paths. Each one distinguishes a key aspect of consultant learning. We now describe each one in turn.

Development paths for trainers

The path from training to consulting

Working collaboratively with a client manager on a consulting project is not nessarily part of traditional trainers' experience; trainers need to learn about the different stages of consultancy and to develop the specific consulting skills associated with each stage. As we shall discuss more fully in Chapter 4, the traditional training cycle and the consulting cycle have many similarities at the level of tasks and procedures. Trainers who are actively involved in all aspects of the training cycle will have experiences, knowledge and skills on which they can build in developing as consultants. However, as recent research shows, most trainers are mainly involved in direct training i.e. face-to-face work with groups of trainees.[2] Training needs analysis, setting training objectives, designing and preparing training courses were also significant aspects of most trainers' work.

Involvement in other activities which could provide valuable developmental experience was less common. These included pre- and post-course individual counselling and coaching, evaluating the effectiveness of training programmes, advising people in the organization and liaising with other functions and outside agencies. Trainers with this experience will find the move to consulting easier than those without.

The approaches we describe in this book assume that the consultant's intention is to promote client learning and development, which implies collaborative work between consultant and client, rather than the consultant as expert prescribing solutions to client problems. Trainers will need to develop the personal skills necessary to form and sustain effective long-term partnerships with a wide variety of clients.

Some trainers will have experience which provides a valuable basis for development along this path, e.g. participative training in which the trainer actively engages trainees in all aspects of the programme, rather than more formal, instructional training methods. Trainers who run any kind of interpersonal skills courses will have developed many of the personal skills needed for client work. Such courses might include influencing skills, negotiating skills, communication skills and assertiveness training.

A theme to which we shall frequently return is the greater ambiguity of consulting work as compared with training. The consultant makes far more use of self than the trainer, who has many more props to hide behind (exercises, theories, lectures etc.). Trainers who have developed their self-knowledge and self-awareness have more confidence in facing the uncertainties and open-endedness of consulting work.

The path from training to learning

In this path there is a shift of responsibility for learning away from the trainer onto the learner. Trainers normally expect to identify training needs and propose training solutions themselves. A learning approach means that the learner is actively involved in defining his or her learning needs and designing ways of meeting them. The learning consultant knows how to help other people learn through self-development. To move in this direction trainers need to acquire a thorough knowledge of how adults learn and of the different preferences people have in the way they learn. They also need to be able to help managers assess their own learning styles and other factors which may facilitate or block learning. Added to this, they need to be able to design learning opportunities that contribute to work task achievement. The consultant's ability to manage relationships with clients needs to be augmented by relationship skills in the role of coach, mentor, counsellor and facilitator.

Once again some trainers will have experience that prepares them for working in this way. Those that use some self-directed learning approaches on training courses will have useful knowledge of self-development methods. Experience as a trainer or participant on unstructured training programmes and action learning sets are all very valuable, as is experience of counselling, all kinds of group work and involvement with networks and support groups.

Chapter 6 will explore this development path in more detail.

The path from individual change to organizational change

A reorientation is necessary. All activities must be looked at in the context of the direction of change and development for the organization as a whole. The organizational change consultant should see each project and each client relationship as a microcosm reflecting wider organizational issues. Trainers developing along this path need to widen their horizons sufficiently to see how models of individual change and development can apply to a whole system, a leap of imagination that requires a sound grasp of diagnostic frameworks and the capacity to gather data continually about the organization.

In order to align individual learning and change with that of the organization, the consultant needs to work at many levels simultaneously, not all of them explicit at any one time. Such consultants also require a high level of personal skill and confidence in order to use themselves as catalysts to enable others to create the future.

Trainers best placed to make this move are likely to have worked closely with people throughout the organization and with all levels of managers to the most senior. Involvement with change programmes, such as departmental restructuring, acquisitions and mergers, customer care programmes, or succession planning, may have given trainers experience of organizational change. At a personal level those trainers who have taken a very proactive approach to their own development and have consciously worked through considerable personal change are the most likely to tread this development path with confidence.

Chapter 8 examines it in greater detail.

Figure 2.2 provides a summary of useful or necessary experience and competences acquired by trainers on each development path. Figure 2.3. combines the concepts of training and consultancy approaches with that of development paths.

Our framework then suggests that each of the consulting approaches requires progress along one, two or all three paths. For example, to work as a training consultant means acquiring the skills of collaborative consultancy; to work as a learning consultant requires in addition the capacity to enable self-

USEFUL/NECESSARY PREVIOUS EXPERIENCE	THE DEVELOPMENT PATHS	COMPETENCES ACQUIRED
Training of trainers; participative training; interpersonal skills training dealing with peoples' real work problems on courses; pre and post course briefings; involvement in all aspects of training cycle (eg. training needs analysis, design, evaluation)	From training to consulting	Becoming more active/visible in the organization; experience in all aspects of the consulting cycle (gaining entry, contracting, data gathering, diagnosis and feedback of recommendations, implementation, follow-up); building collaborative relationships with clients; enhanced training design skills; greater business awareness
Experience of organizations and work other than as a trainer; running self development/ self directed activities on courses; experience of personal awareness training (as trainer or participant); experience of counselling/ therapy; running unstructured training; group-work experience; working with teams; experience of action learning/networks/ support groups	From training to learning	Recognizing training as only one way of developing people; understanding how adults learn; enabling self/mutual development; developing managers as developers of others; able to work as mentor, coach, counsellor, facilitator, as well as trainer; designing learning events which are directly productive for work tasks; identifying/creating learning resources
Proactive development of own career; thorough knowledge of own organization; experience/knowledge of different organizational forms; team building; working with senior mgt; working with whole dept./ small org; curiosity/interest in wider issues (eg social, economic, political, business trends)	From individual change to organizational change	Designing development which supports org. change taking a whole system perspective; taking a long-term view; ability to conceptualize about complex change; facilitating organizational activities; working with all levels of management; using self as a catalyst; working with org. culture, purpose and vision

Figure 2.2 The development paths

development; to work as an organization change consultant requires in addition to both of these, the capacity to work with the total system.

The implications of this framework are:

1. The choice of consulting approach defines the choice of development paths.
2. The choice of consulting approach for any particular assignment depends on:
   - the client's needs and expectations,
   - the ability of the consultant to see the opportunities inherent in the situation,
   - the consultant's contracting skills, particularly in challenging the parameters of the assignment as it develops.

The framework provides a model for the rest of the book as can be seen in Figure 2.3.

We shall start in Chapter 3 by describing certain fundamental training attitudes which need to be dropped for development along any of the paths.

Notes

1. Bennis, W.G. *ORGANIZATION DEVELOPMENT: ITS NATURE, ORIGINS AND PROSPECTS*, Addison-Wesley 1969.
2. Bennett, R. (ed.) *IMPROVING TRAINER EFFECTIVENESS*, Gower 1988.

27

Figure 2.3   A model for trainer development

3   The Personal Challenge

Experience as a management trainer provides an excellent basis for developing as a consultant, but it is also true that certain characteristics and approaches which contribute to success as a trainer can militate against effectiveness as a consultant. Unfortunately it is often easier to learn new ways than relinquish old ones. Many people treasure those attitudes and methods on which they have based their current sense of competence; they cling to them for support in new situations where their self-confidence seems more fragile. Sometimes the familiar skills will stand them in good stead, and in subsequent chapters we will consider the skills trainers can build on as they develop among the three paths we indicated in Chapter 2; but in this chapter we concentrate on those aspects of being a trainer which are best left behind because they are inappropriate for the different challenges of consulting work.

This process of letting go will be less or more difficult depending on individual experience and inclination. In working with a wide range of people in transition between training and consulting, we have identified some common problems in letting go:

- Letting go of performing, being the centre of attention and expecting 'applause'.
- Letting go of a clear-cut power position and control of events.

- Letting go of predictability and being well prepared for what comes next.

These three aspects of training – performing, power and predictability – are closely woven together in the relationships set up in the training room between a trainer and a group of course members. Learning to handle them successfully is part of a trainer's development and is likely to be a source of satisfaction and pleasure in the job. We look now at each in turn and consider how they may become a source of ineffectiveness in contexts other than training.

Letting go of performing

The notion of performance involves one or more people being active while others observe. An effective performer commands the attention and interest of an audience. Even when there is interaction between performer and audience, it is recognized by all as part of the performance. It is then the successful performer who is congratulated and applauded for achieving a good rapport.

Trainers develop the capacity to perform most obviously in order to give theory presentations, e.g. formal lectures using overhead slides or informal inputs made spontaneously with the help of a flipchart. After a lecture the trainer may invite questions or lead a discussion. He or she may encourage participation during a more informal theory input. Applause comes from course members in the form of comments like, 'You made that concept so interesting, I wasn't bored for a minute', or 'I really enjoyed the way you presented those ideas, you made it so easy to grasp'.

Although this way is the most obvious, we would argue that trainers perform in several other ways, as follows:

- When they engage in any activity in order to illustrate or demonstrate to course members some behaviour or skill, e.g. stepping into a role-play exercise to show a course member what a more assertive posture might look like. (Applause: 'Oh, I see what you mean. Yes, that works much better'.)

- When they draw together the threads at the end of an exercise so that everything suddenly falls into place. (Applause: 'When you said that, things really began to make sense to me'.)
- When they select a few moments from a closed circuit television recording that illustrate a point they have already made, e.g. the effect of closed questions in an interview. (Applause: Rueful laughter.)

Many trainers would probably recognize these examples as part of their repertoire, but in some situations trainers may be less conscious of their performing role.

The benefits of 'performing' in training, as we have defined it, are linked to traditional goals of teaching people knowledge and training them in the skills they need for effectiveness in their work. The trainer as performer seeks to keep people stimulated and interested, to encourage them to be receptive to new ideas and different ways of doing things and to get across salient points with maximum impact. Usually such trainers are well liked by course members, who enjoy their courses and find the material memorable. They will be deemed highly effective in their role, yet we are suggesting that these particular skills can be very unhelpful in many aspects of consulting, particularly when working with managers on live issues in their organizational setting. This becomes clear when we look at some other consequences of performing as a trainer:

1. *The interest of the subject matter is linked with the skill of the performer.* Course members are interested as much because the trainer 'made it interesting' as because of the relevance of the material or their own interest in it.
2. *Being a member of the audience is a passive role.* Course members expect the trainer to entertain and stimulate them.
3. *Audience participation is stage-managed by the performer.* The trainer leads discussions, briefs for syndicate work, suggests exercises in pairs or trios.
4. *Performers sometimes do not like being upstaged.* The trainer rarely takes a genuinely low profile position in the training group.
5. *Performers are sometimes seen as larger than life, the subject*

of the audience's idealized fantasies (they may even begin to see themselves that way). Trainers 'know what they are talking about', 'know how to handle a training group' and if they make a mistake, use it to illustrate how to handle making mistakes!

6. *Performers want applause from the audience and use it to measure their success.* Trainers often collect feedback sheets at the end of the course. They want them to be positive, and if not, may feel downhearted and unappreciated.

7. *People remember a well constructed performance.* Course members may well memorize material covered by a good performer-trainer. They may or may not leave with internalized learning.

Consider the case of John, a consultant, at a meeting with a group of client managers. He may be discussing the design of a training course (training consultant) or facilitating a team meeting (learning or organization change consultant). John until recently, has been an effective trainer, who has enjoyed performing. There are aspects of this situation where John's skills and experience may not help him:

- It is not his job to win his clients' attention throughout and make things interesting for them. On the contrary, he needs to help them uncover what is of real interest, relevance and concern to them. He needs to be working with *their* data rather than his.
- He is not there to perform as a consultant while his clients watch. The more active and self-empowered his clients are, the more successful will be the implementation of any consulting assignment.
- He is not there to stage-manage the interaction between people. He needs to be able to recognize the actual dynamics in the situation, help others to recognize this and to facilitate real contact and engagement.
- He is not the star in the production. He needs to be comfortable with many different roles, some of them low in visibility. He needs to be able to work implicitly out of the limelight, where his contribution is less obvious, as well as in the glare of centre-stage.

- He needs to demonstrate genuine, authentic behaviour rather than larger-than-life qualities. He needs to be trusted more than admired. The relation of performer to audience is essentially symbiotic, whereas consultants work towards client independence. 'We can do it without you.'
- He will probably receive less overt appreciation and applause for his contribution; perhaps some of it will not even be recognized. He will need to develop other less external ways of rewarding himself in his work.
- Since as a consultant he is not there to teach or train people but to help them learn, problem-solve and develop, his skills in helping people memorize things will not be sufficient. Providing instant understanding, making sense of everything for everyone, may not help anyone learn, least of all himself.

So when the meeting runs into difficulties, and especially when John believes that the managers are looking to him to justify his presence as a consultant, he may be tempted to intervene in ways that were appropriate for the training room. He may want to stand up, grab a pen, and talk about blocks to group effectiveness. He may want to give extensive feedback to the chair about her leadership style. These interventions may make good training points and have high impact but they may be less useful than a few brief comments designed to enable the group to continue to make progress.

Letting go of a clear-cut power position

The link between this section and the previous one is control. Performing successfully comes with a strong element of control, whereas effective consulting often means being willing to relinquish control.

We look first of all at the power that trainers have, as temporary leaders of the training group. In our experience trainers tend to play down the position power they draw on, preferring to focus on their more personal power base (skills, knowledge, personality). But if they do that, they are being wilfully blind to the control they exert over so many aspects of a training course. Perhaps they lay down conditions of eligibility for the programme, they decide the room layout to suit their purposes, they select which materials and facilities are and are not available to participants, they decide on a timetable and a sequence of activities, they may ask a person to leave a course if they believe them to be disrupting the learning of others. In comparison course members arriving on a training programme feel little or no position power, and much of their early behaviour demonstrates the power differential. Most trainers acquire far more than a theoretical understanding of the stages of group development (dependence, counter-dependence, independence, interdependence)[1] through the repeated experience of retaining power or engaging in power struggles or sharing power, depending on the objectives of the training course.

Perhaps the most vivid illustration of the trainer's power is what happens when trainers choose *not* to exercise the power of their position (by asking the course members what they want to do or by not giving answers or direction). Unless there has been considerable negotiation about power and roles, the trainer will be acting directly contrary to the expectations of course members. After all, only those with power are in a position to choose or give it up or delegate it, as when a trainer asks course members to plan and manage a day of self-directed workshop activities.

In comparison with the trainer, a consultant does not have ready access to position power as a source of influence. Indeed most definitions of the term consultant explicitly exclude the authority to control. Consultants really do have to rely on the effective use of themselves, their personal and consulting skills, in order to influence their clients. This is not to say that consultants do not deal all the time with issues of power. Peter Block suggests that concerns about control or vulnerability are the two major stumbling blocks in consultant—client relationships.[2] For this reason, we believe that those trainers who have never fully faced the realities of their own power position in the training room and understood how they use (and sometimes misuse) it, will be less able to relinquish control as consultants in order to see and handle effectively the different power issues they will face. They may at worst construe all events in the same terms as the power relationships they were familiar with in the training room.

There are two other relevant aspects to this question of letting go of well defined power and control. One concerns territory, the other the explicit use of theory and exercises.

Trainers usually work on their own territory, whether at a training centre or training department. Even when using a hotel, trainers usually make sure they are familiar with the venue and have organized the layout of furniture before course members arrive.

The situation for consultants is quite different. They usually meet their clients on the latter's home ground. They have to gain entry and establish a role for themselves by good contracting. A trainer plays an important part in establishing the unwritten rules, but a consultant seeks to uncover and understand the norms of the client system.

Finally, one of the ways that trainers can exercise control is through the use of theory and exercises. Theory can promote understanding and exercises can provide opportunity for practice. At the same time they may also be ways in which the trainer seeks to prevent difficulties surfacing in the group because he or she feels unable to handle the issues. In such instances the theory or exercise intervention is one way a trainer can control the situation. On a training course, particularly one where relationships are short-term, this can be effective and the trainer will, in any case, probably be meeting course members' expectations. But the consultant working with managers in their work context does not have these 'props' and reaching for them when conflict emerges may cloud issues and leave important organizational problems festering. It may be vital for the consultant not to 'handle' (in other words, control) the situation but to enable confusion, tension or conflict to be faced openly, without escape routes.

Letting go of predictability

There are many ways in which the trainer's life has more certainty and security built into it compared with that of the consultant. A few examples will illustrate this.

Workload

A series of training courses can be planned ahead in a logical manner, allowing time for preparation and other related activities. The workload is sequential, with a trainer running one course at a time, completing each assignment before starting the next. A consultant has to let go of this sort of certainty in order to juggle several incomplete projects simultaneously. Timescales and commitments may need to be renegotiated as projects are extended, expanded into new areas or curtailed. Diary planning has to be flexible enough to cope with change and the unexpected. Above all, the consultant needs to be able to live permanently with 'work in progress' rather than the satisfaction of a series of finished assignments.

Structure

Training courses follow a structured sequence of events that has been designed beforehand. Even when the course allows considerable flexibility with self-directed work by participants, the trainers are usually drawing on a pool of known resources and possibilities. The simulated nature of activities on structured training courses removes the unpredictability, politics and extra intensity of emotional involvement which occur when live problems are being dealt with in the workplace. Although consultants have many opportunities to use their design skills, they will also have to work in situations where they really know no more than their clients about what will happen next.

Relationships

The trainer knows how long the relationship with trainees will last, because the length of the course, and any pre- or post-course work which has been built around it, are laid down. The relationship between consultant and client is much more variable. It may last hours or years. Also the nature of the trainer--trainee relationship is defined by the relative lack of ambiguity in the two roles. The consultant has to negotiate his or her role and the nature of the relationship with clients, within a far wider range of possibilities and mutual expectations. There will be

questions such as the following. What is the structure of hierarchical relationships with which I will have to deal? Who are the
different parties within the client system with whom I will need to
contract? Who is the real decision-maker ?

In summary we are suggesting that, in becoming consultants,
trainers need to be willing to let go of a number of things they
may well value:

- The pleasure of performing well in front of an audience.
- The security of a well defined power position in the training
  room.
- The advantage of working on 'home' territory.
- The safeguard of being able to use theory and exercise to
  control situations.
- The predictability of a planned, sequenced workload.
- The relative simplicity of the trainer – trainee relationship.
- The luxury of working one step removed from the cauldron
  of organizational politics.

There is of course another side to all this. There are many trainers
who see consultancy as an opportunity to let go of irksome,
draining or dissatisfying aspects of their work. They would see
the 'luxury' of reigning in the training room, isolated from the
work context of managers, as a liability that keeps them removed
from the mainstream of organizational life and prevents them
from exerting greater influence for change. They would point to
the strain of building short-term working relationships with
group after group of trainees, rather than having the opportunity
to develop long-term trust and collaboration with client
managers. They would gladly forgo the sense of completion that
comes from positive end-of-course feedback and a set of good
action plans if they could have instead the chance to see learning
being applied and its actual impact on individual, team or
organizational effectiveness. Finally, they may be happy to
exchange the adrenalin of performance for the excitement and
challenge of seeing live work problems being confronted and
resolved over time.

Notes

1. Weber R. C. 'The Group: A Cycle from Birth to Death', in Porter L. and Mohr B. (eds), *READING BOOK FOR HUMAN RELATIONS TRAINING*, NTL Institute 1982.
2. Block P. *FLAWLESS CONSULTING: A GUIDE TO GETTING YOUR EXPERTISE USED*, Learning Concepts 1981.

4 From Training to Consulting

In Chapter 2 we identified three development paths for trainers becoming consultants. Each of these expands the trainer's work in different but overlapping directions. Common to all three is the need to develop consulting skills for managing relationships with clients. For training consultants this is the main development path.

Many excellent books on the principles of consultancy have already been written and we do not intend to cover the ground again. For the reader who would like a single reference in this area we would recommend *Flawless Consulting* by Peter Block.[1] What we propose to do in this chapter, as elsewhere in the book, is to approach consulting from the perspective of those with a background in training. In the last chapter we discussed what trainers need to leave behind in the transition to consulting; now we shall concentrate on the competences they can build on and new areas for development.

The definition that we find most useful describes a consultant as someone who is in a position to influence change but who has no direct authority to implement change programmes. A client is any person or group whom the consultant seeks to influence. As we argued in Chapter 3, the trainer does have a form of temporary authority over trainees in the training room although trainers vary in the degree to which they use or even acknowledge this authority. Nevertheless both trainers and consultants cannot be really effective without developing the capacity to influence through the personal qualities, expertise and skills, which form their real power base.

The training cycle v the consulting cycle

Both training and consulting can be described as systematic approaches involving a number of phases. Six of these are usually identified in the basic training cycle:

THE TRAINING CYCLE
Identifying training needs
Setting training objectives
Selecting methods of validation and evaluation
Designing the training course
Running the training course
Carrying out validation and evaluation

Readers may come across variations of the consulting cycle, but most practitioners would broadly agree with the following stages:

THE CONSULTING CYCLE
Gaining entry
Agreeing a working contract
Data collection, analysis and diagnosis
Formulating proposals
Feedback to clients and decision to act
Implementation
Follow-up

Both models are cycles in that information generated in the last stage may signal a return to earlier stages. It is more appropriate to identify separate, well defined steps in the training cycle, as each stage should be completed before moving on to the next. In consultancy there is more often overlap between the stages and recycling within the cycle. Already this points to the greater ambiguity of consulting work.

Table 4.1 compares the two models. The arrows show where the training cycle has potential for preparing trainers for consulting work.

Table 4.1

Training cycle	Consulting cycle
	Gaining entry
	Agreeing a working contract
Identifying training needs ⟶	Data collection, analysis and diagnosis
Setting training objectives	
Selecting methods of validation and evaluation ⟶	Formulating proposals
Designing the training course	
	Feedback to clients and decision to act
Running the training course ⟶	Implementation
Carrying out validation and evaluation ⟶	Follow-up

Juxtaposing the two cycles in this way gives us a rationale for the remainder of this chapter. First we shall look briefly at the competences which a trainer familiar with all aspects of the training cycle can bring to consulting work. Secondly we shall examine aspects of the consulting cycle for which trainers may be less well prepared. These centre on the need for continuous collaboration with clients throughout an assignment.

Competences gained from experience of the training cycle

The methods typically used to carry out a training needs survey provide many opportunies for developing useful tools and skills for the data collection stage of consulting. Trainers may examine job descriptions and person specifications or analyse the outcomes of appraisal systems. They may conduct a series of interviews with managers and their staff, design and administer questionnaires or use critical incident analysis.

Transferable competences:
Contacts across functions and throughout the hierarchy.
Knowledge of the organization.
Interviewing skills.
Observation skills.
Analytical skills.
Diagnostic skills (in terms of identifying training needs).

The next three stages of the training cycle involve the preparation of training programmes, from setting training objectives and designing a course, to the writing or selection of course materials. In effect the trainer produces a 'proposal' for meeting the training needs identified.

Transferable competences:
Knowledge of various rationales, models and methodologies which underpin training design and training evaluation.
Creative design skills.

The next stage involves organizing and running a series of training courses. This is the implementation stage.

Transferable competences:
Planning and organizing skills in allocating staff resources, collating materials, arranging venues, managing budgets etc.
Presentation skills.
A wide range of interpersonal and process skills needed to run a training course.
Understanding of and ability to manage group dynamics.

Some courses may involve pre-course briefing and post-course follow-up with participants, while those that involve more intensive personal learning may require the trainer to offer extra one-to-one support during the course.

Transferable competences:
Feedback skills.
Coaching skills.
Counselling skills.

Finally if methods of validation and evaluation involve more than end-of-course feedback sheets, then trainers will have the opportunity to assess the impact of the training in the work situation. This will mean returning to some of the activities carried out in stage 1 of the cycle.

A word of warning here. In our experience there are many trainers for whom the training cycle is more a theoretical concept than a true description of their work. This is borne out by the survey to which we have already referred in Chapter 2,[2] which showed that 'direct training' (i.e. stage 5 running training courses), was the main element of trainers' work. It is thus perfectly possible for trainers not to have developed the full range of competences listed here. Trainers who have gained experience in *all* the stages of the training cycle are better prepared for undertaking consulting work.

The nature of this development path

Looking again at the comparison between the two cycles, we see three stages in the consulting cycle which do not have parallels in the training cycle. These are the first two stages (gaining entry and agreeing working contracts) and stage 5 (feedback to clients and decision to act). We explain the differences in the following way.

As functional specialists, trainers do not need to gain entry to client managers, or to negotiate working contracts with them. It is their functional responsibility to identify and meet training needs in the organization and it is perfectly legitimate for the training department to make a unilateral decision to embark on a training needs survey. In other words, they can step straight into the data collection stage and are quite likely to take responsibility for deciding what data to collect, how to collect it and what to do with it. It is then perfectly possible for trainers to carry out the next three stages of the training cycle under the auspices of the training department, drawing solely on their own expertise.

The result of their efforts is likely to be the publication of a brochure of training courses, complete with dates, objectives, outline content and guidelines for eligibility for each course. Implementation of the courses then goes ahead as participants are nominated. Implicitly managers 'agree' to the proposals for the courses by attending them, but the decision to go ahead and run the programmes has been made by the training department.

Trainers do think of line managers *in general* as their clients, but as they become internal consultants, they need to negotiate working relationships with individual managers who will be the sponsoring clients for each consulting project. Trainers' experience of the training cycle may lead them to have a limited and limiting view of their role in this relationship; they may be more likely to adopt an expert position. This has been described as the 'physician's approach', i.e. the client presents symptoms and the consultant conducts an examination, makes a diagnosis and prescribes a remedy. The client remains relatively passive and dependent until the point at which he or she decides whether to implement the recommendations. At this point the position is reversed as the consultant waits to see if the client metaphorically tears up the prescription, pretends to accept it but never takes the pills, completes only part of the prescribed treatment or takes the medicine and, depending on the results, views the 'doctor' as a saviour or a quack.

It is now widely recognized that expert consulting is effective mainly for short-term problem-solving: it is characteristic of consulting in technical fields such as marketing, finance, computer technology and so on. It does not produce a lasting, self-sustaining change for the client. For this reason when we talk about consulting in this book, we shall be advocating a collaborative approach. This is because we are writing about consultancy whose prime purpose is client learning and development, whatever technical aspects to the assignment there may be.

To collaborate means to work together to create a partnership based on mutual trust and mutual recognition of each other's different contributions. Such an approach is characterized by three factors:

1. A relationship between consultant and client which is based on personal equality, regardless of differences in specialized knowledge, skill, age or hierarchical position.

2. A strong, jointly agreed working contract which is open to renegotiation by both parties.
3. Client involvement in all stages of the project.

In the remainder of this chapter we discuss these three characteristics in some detail, giving guidelines for trainers wanting to work as collaborative consultants.

Creating equal partnerships with clients

In Chapter 3 we discussed the nature of trainer–trainee relationships in the training room. The situation unfortunately arouses memories of school and echoes of teacher–pupil relationships. If trainers consciously or unconsciously reinforce this memory, then they may well invoke in course members a range of compliant, rebellious, passive or competitive behaviours in response. Some trainers will have learnt to recognize and accept the underlying dynamics of their relationships with training groups and will take great satisfaction in encouraging collaborative relationships as the course progresses. Some may do this implicitly, others, because of the objectives of the course, may do so more explicitly. Some of the issues, and certainly the skills needed to handle them, are just as valid when we look at the possible dynamics of consultant–client relationships.

For the internal consultant the seeds of personal inequality may lie in:

- A difference in hierarchical status between consultant and client manager.
- A previous relationship on a different basis such as trainer-course member or boss–subordinate.
- An organizational culture which includes line-specialist friction.

Both internal and external consultants may also have to contend with other issues in building relationships with their clients such as:

- Clients' fixed preconceptions about trainers or consultants.

- Consultants' fixed preconceptions about managers.
- Consultants feeling under pressure to prove themselves.
- Clients wanting to abdicate responsibility to a consultant.
- Consultants over-eager to land an assignment.
- Clients who want to use consultants as temporary extra resources at their disposal.
- Unwilling clients being pressurized into using a consultant by their boss.
- Consultants' unexpressed anxieties about making a good impression, about being a possible scapegoat, about making a success of a project, about being helpful.
- Clients unexpressed anxieties about being conned, about losing face, about staying in control, about avoiding 'sensitive' areas.

Many trainers will recognize these as process issues in the 'task, procedure and process' model of human interaction represented in Figure 4.1.

Figure 4.1   Human interaction model

The *task* is the work that people set out to complete together, e.g. consultant and client meet to establish the goals of a consulting project. This is their task in this instance.

The *procedures* are the methods people choose for organizing themselves in achieving the task. For example, $1\frac{1}{2}$ hours are allocated for a meeting. The client starts by outlining his or her thoughts. After some questioning and discussion with the consultant five points are logged on a white board. The client agrees to expand these points in writing and send a copy to the consultant. The consultant agrees to write a proposal for the way in which the consulting assignment could progress, for discussion with the client at their next meeting.

The *process* is the underlying feelings and motivations people bring to the task and to each other, e.g. whether consultant and/or client is scared, excited, defensive, suspicious, impatient, etc; whether either feels that his or her neck is on the line. Whether each believes the other is being honest.

As Figure 4.1 shows, *task* is the most accessible and obvious level in the interaction, the tip of the iceberg. It is the ostensible reason for the interaction. The procedures may be explicitly agreed or may emerge, partly in response to the demands of the task and partly as the way the process level is revealed. The *process* level is the least accessible, but is the foundation on which the task is built. As such, it governs the strength or weakness of the other layers and gives colour, life and character to the task and procedures. It is important to deal with process right from the outset of meetings with clients. It is easier to build an equal relationship to begin with than break the mould of an unequal one later on.

The following are the key components in the process of establishing equal relationships with clients:

1. Having a strong base of self-esteem.
2. Listening to clients.
3. Refusing to be rushed through the contracting stage.
4. Expressing consultant's wants for the project as well as finding out what the client wants.
5. Paying attention to any feelings of unease experienced during early meetings.
6. Being willing to ask direct questions.
7. Giving and eliciting feedback on the progress of the relationship.

Let us look more closely at each in turn.

Self-esteem

For trainers moving into consultancy, leaving behind the security of a familiar role, self-confidence may be at a low ebb. Before meeting a potential client it may help trainers to remember the wide range of skill and experience they already have – the transferable competences outlined earlier in this chapter. Furthermore, they should be able to recognize the type of client remarks that deflate their self-confidence and consider possible responses. The best response is to maintain an attitude of curiosity rather than become defensive, e.g.:

Client: We've tried something like that before and it was a disaster.
Consultant: What happened? What do we need to pay attention to this time, in order to avoid similar problems?

Client: How much do you really understand about the pressures we're under here?
Consultant: What else do you think it's important that I understand?

Although consultants offer specialist knowledge and skills, they do not need to put themselves under pressure to come up with instant answers to everything. On the contrary, a consultant who wants to appear to know all the answers risks encouraging a relationship in which the client accepts or rejects the consultant's proposals but has no ownership in them.

Listening to the client

Often new consultants believe they will need to impress potential clients by selling themselves and their services. However, what clients most want is understanding of their concerns, needs and priorities from someone who is realistic and confident about how he or she can help. The main skills in early meetings therefore are good listening, asking good questions and the capacity to express understanding of the client's view of the project, including its special features and the client's desired outcomes. Very often consultants establish credibility with clients at this stage not by offering anything new but simply by reflecting back accurately what has been said to them. True collaboration in consultancy means working together on the *client's* concerns, not the consultant's favourite intervention. For trainers this may mean not using jargon to sound clever and not distorting what the client is saying to fit a training intervention they know how to run.

Contracting well

Clients who pride themselves on being action managers in a culture that rewards this will put themselves and others under pressure to get on and do something fast. Resist this temptation until a solid working contract has been agreed. At this point the consultants' knowledge of what needs to be covered in each phase of the consulting cycle may be the particular contribution they bring to the collaboration. Being assertive about this is one way of establishing personal equality in the early meetings. Consultants who find themselves talking about the design for an intervention at the first meeting with a client are clearly being seduced or bullied into premature action, or else are themselves uncomfortable about resolving the process issues of the contracting stage. We shall say more about this later in this chapter.

Negotiating wants and offers

It is a common error for consultants to concentrate exclusively on finding out what their clients want from them. Although obviously important, this can lead to a one-sided, unequal relationship. At one extreme the consultant becomes a Uriah Heap character, obsequiously striving to satisfy the client's wishes. At the other extreme the consultant can be in danger of becoming a super-hero, promising too much and allowing unrealistic expectations. Balance is achieved by the consultant's willingness to talk about such things as:

- What I can and cannot do.
- What my own values are.

- What I will *need* from you, the client, to ensure success in the project.
- What I *want* from you, the client, in order to work at my best.
- What I want from the project to meet my own need for satisfaction and achievement.

Expressing views in these areas gives the opportunity for consultant and client to negotiate as equals about what they want from, and what they can offer to, the project and each other. Obviously in order to do this, consultants need to have thought carefully about what collaboration means to them and what it is appropriate for them to ask for, e.g.:

'Before I begin I would like you to brief the staff I shall be interviewing about the background to this project'.
'I would like you to include me in that meeting you are arranging with X'.
'I want us to agree some form of joint evaluation of this project about 6 months after its completion.'
'I think your involvement in the team-building will be very important. How much time are you willing to give to this?'

Noticing feelings of unease

Vague feelings of unease or discomfort are sure signs that important process issues are not being dealt with. It is tempting for consultants to ignore or dismiss them if they are over-anxious to get work, or keen to please their clients at all costs or reluctant to rock the boat; but we have learnt that it is never worth while. One must recognize the unease, pinpoint its cause and consciously choose when and how to raise the issue.

We were once invited by another consultant to consider the possibility of becoming part of a European consultant team which her client, a multi-national company based in America, was assembling. Attracted by the apparent glamour of the assignment, we were keen to become involved and travelled to a location on the continent to take part in a pilot programme.

The consultants our colleague had recommended were to participate in the programme and then be involved in design meetings for progressing the project in Europe. We were welcomed warmly and in the midst of the general bonhomie it was all too easy to submerge the vague doubts we had about the basis for our involvement, which had 'been sorted out' between the client and our American colleague. On the final day it emerged that the event was being used as a way of assessing the consultants. The anger, defensiveness and mistrust that was generated at that meeting severely strained relationships and was a setback for both consultants *and* clients.

On later reflection we knew that we had suspected the truth in our hearts but had colluded in not facing it. This is a fairly extreme example, but all twinges of unease, if denied, instead of explored, weaken the ground on which really collaborative relationships can be built.

Asking direct questions

Following on from the last point, we have found that consultants can avoid colluding with their clients if they ask seemingly naive or awkward questions. It is interesting to speculate on the extent to which clients really want to change things when they call in consultants. What has been learned about the nature of change is that it involves at least some degree of loss, pain and confusion before new direction is established. So it is perfectly possible that consultants and clients may seek each other out in order to create the appearance of change while actually avoiding it. The consultant's willingness to confront issues in a timely way is one signal of a healthy rather than collusive relationship. The skills involved may well have been acquired by trainers who use constructive challenge to help people learn by, for example:

- Asking questions that are simple and direct.
- Watching out for redefinition, i.e. a different question being answered than the one asked.
- Quietly persisting in asking the question again, immediately or later.

- Tolerating silence and giving the client time to respond rather than answering the question oneself or defending having asked it.

Awkward questions are often needed to explore the opposite of whatever is being comfortably talked about. For example:

- Doubts and risks when the client is only expressing confidence and optimism.
- Short-term implications when only long-term issues are being discussed.
- Other parties involved when the client is talking as if this is a personal pet project.
- What the client actually *wants* when the discussion has concentrated on what ought to happen or what the situation demands.

In other words, this is where a consultant needs to stay out of the client's frame of reference as well as being able to step into it.

Exchanging feedback

Since the quality of the consultant–client relationship is such an important part of consulting, it is a good idea to be able to talk about it. Relationships can become productive most quickly if both sides are operating not with assumptions about each other's reactions but with real information about the effect they are having on one another. This is an area where trainers usually have skills, as long as they are accustomed to *exchanging* feedback rather than giving it most of the time or only asking for it formally at the end of a course. Consultants might want to find out what led the client to want to work with him or her in particular, to ask in what ways he or she is being helpful or unhelpful, and to review the effectiveness of the collaboration at regular intervals. It also means deciding when and how to give such information to the client.

Agreeing an effective working contract

This involves consultant and client agreeing what it is they aim to achieve together, how they are going to set out doing this and who is responsible for what. This agreement is not intended to force compliance between the parties, as in a legal contract. Its purpose is to clarify conditions that will give the project the greatest chance of success. Because the tasks of the contracting stage sound straightforward and obvious enough, it is easy to underestimate the care needed to contract well. Probably all consultants would agree that problems arising in later stages of an assignment can be traced back to poor initial contracting or failure to renegotiate the contract as circumstances change.

Training contracts

Trainers often do not spend a great deal of time explicitly contracting with trainees. A training course is published, with dates, aims and outline of contents and methods. In doing this trainers are stating their side of the contract. In arriving for the course trainees implicitly accept the contract, but, as many trainers know to their cost, this very limited type of contracting gives no guarantee that there is real understanding between the parties about their expectations of one another.

Some trainers seek to overcome this by engaging in some further contracting at the start of a course. They may outline the course objectives again, and explain their role and their expectations of course members. Unfortunately they are likely to get very quick acceptance of whatever they propose. At this stage of a course trainees are all too willing to be dependent (and even insistent) on the trainer taking leadership.

Some trainers go further in encouraging an exchange of expectations about the course, devoting time to agreeing which ones they are and are not able or willing to meet, and seeking the same information from participants; but it is in many ways already too late for this dialogue. The course has started, and the area open to change by negotiation is inevitably limited. Even when trainers take care to provide extensive briefing notes for participants or arrange to speak with them before the course, this is less about contracting than about selection.

Compared with consulting relationships, the lack of solid contracting that characterizes so many training courses can be tolerated because:

1. The parameters of the relationship between trainer and trainee are relatively clear-cut and short-term.
2. The task they are working on together does not involve live organizational issues, so that less is at stake.

None the less lack of clarity and mutual understanding about aims and responsibilities does lead to all sort of problems on courses:

- 'Difficult' course members.
- Rejection of the trainer and/or the course material.
- Dissatisfaction for trainer and trainees.
- Wasted time and resources.

Trainers who have experienced these problems, no matter how well planned their courses, need to appreciate that strong contracts in consulting are even more important.

Consulting contracts[3]

It may take one or several meetings to arrive at a consulting contract. Some relationships will never progress to this stage. Some perfectly legitimate outcomes from the first meeting with a client could be:

- Consultant and client agree *not* to embark on a project together and both understand why not.
- Initial contact is made and the door is open for further visits but the client is still a potential rather than an actual client.
- Consultant agrees to write a proposal for working with the client (draft contract) to be discussed at a further meeting.
- Consultant and client agree the basis of a contract. Perhaps dates are to be decided. A phone call or letter is needed to confirm the contract.

- All aspects of a working contract are agreed at the meeting.

Although a written contract is not necessary, it is very helpful in testing mutual understanding. (Is what *you* think I said the same as what *I* think I said and did we mean the same by these words anyway?)

There is no single way of writing a contract – it may be informal or formal, a lengthy document, a letter or just a set of points. Subsequent chapters give some examples. The elements that need to be covered are:

1. Brief summary of the background and need for the project (the context).
2. The aims and objectives of the project.
3. Who is involved and who is responsible for doing what.
4. The agreed first steps.
5. Timescales and fees.

There are two areas we would like to discuss further. One is the difficulty of defining who is actually the client and the second is the often awkward subject of consultant time and how to charge for it.

Who is the client?

Trainers have no problem defining who their trainees are. Everyone who has enrolled on a course is a course member and the primary contract is between trainer and trainees for the duration of the course. Sometimes there are complications when trainers are expected to report back in some way to nominating managers or other interested parties, but in our experience most trainers resist being placed in this position, arguing that it does not produce a helpful learning climate. It is also true that trainers are under contract to their own managers in the training department but this type of contract is the same as that between all employees and their managers and is supervisory in nature, unlike contracts negotiated where there are no direct hierarchical relationships.

Consultants need to contract in some way with a number of

different people on any particular assignment. They are interested in finding out:

- Who is the person with the real authority to commission the consultant's services? This person as the sponsor has the ultimate say in which and how many resources are available for the project. He or she may or may not be the first person that the consultant meets regarding the project.
- Who is the main person with whom the consultant will collaborate (the liaison)? If this is not the same person as the sponsor, a clear three-way contract will be needed.
- Are the sponsor and/or the liaison beneficiaries of the project, i.e. are they committed to its outcomes or is there a less visible beneficiary exerting pressure somewhere?
- Is there a target group on whom the project is intended to impact? The contract with the sponsor needs to be clear about how this group will become involved in the project.
- Are there other parties who will be affected in some way by the project? To what extent, when and how do they need to be involved?

The consultant's job is to reconnoitre this territory, establish who is who and have clear agreements about how he or she is going to work with the different members of the client system. Such a job may be easier for the internal consultant who is familiar with the formal and informal structure of the organization than the external consultant, who needs to gather this information in the early stages by asking direct questions and not taking anything for granted.

Another aspect of reconnoitring the territory is finding out whether other consultants are or have been involved with the client system. One colleague told us how he undertook extensive work on a project only to be told his proposals nearly duplicated those of an earlier consultant. If he had found out that a previous consulting intervention had been made, he could have saved a lot of time and, probably more importantly, realized that the real problem was a reluctance in the client system to take productive action. They preferred to keep researching the problem than actually to implement change.

Estimating consultant time

This aspect of contracting can be an awkward one for both consultants and clients. It is one that external consultants cannot avoid; nor can those growing numbers of internal consultants who, operating from a profit-centre, are charging for their services. We would argue that even if this is not the case, internal consultants need to place a value on their own time in order to contract professionally and to have a basis for assessing different assignments, choosing between them and organizing their workload. Internal consultants who do not contract for their time can easily overcommit themselves, allow unrealistic timescales or undertake projects that are not viable in business terms.

The points we make below about fees are therefore also relevant for talking about consultant time as a finite and valuable resource, whether or not pound signs are attached. In fact consultant time is not what the client is really buying, rather it is the quality of the consultant's concentrated attention during that time.

Deciding on fee levels   It is important for consultants to have a basis for charging fees that takes into account market rates, their own level of experience and the sort of consultancy services they offer. For trainers there may need to be a mental switch in charging for themselves and their time rather than charging for a course or places on a course. This is a vital distinction. For example, someone selling training packages may quote an all-in fee for running a course for a fixed number of participants, with associated meetings and other preparation included – a sales rather than a consulting approach. What a consultant should assess is the amount of time needed to undertake all or part of a proposed project, and multiply it by a daily fee. Deciding on a daily rate enables consultants to be clear and assertive in stating their fees at the outset of a contract with a potential client. The cost of the project is then allied to what the client wants to achieve and how much time the consultant estimates it will take. If the cost is too much, the client can consider:

–   Using a consultant with a lower fee rate.

- Questioning the consultant's estimate of time needed for different aspects of the project.
- Reviewing the scope of the project and setting more limited objectives.
- Agreeing to a pilot or first stage, after which further work can be agreed.

Dealing with fees in this way enables both parties to handle more comfortably the underlying anxieties that talking about time and money can arouse. For example these could be:

Client	Consultant
Am I being taken advantage of?	Am I being taken advantage of?
How do I know what I'm buying?	Am I selling myself short?
Should I haggle?	Will I be seen as over-rating myself?

Fixed rate Trainers who see running courses as their main work can be tempted to charge a lower rate for other sorts of activity. Charging less for data collection, interviews, design and follow-up work encourages all parties to devalue these aspects of the consultant's contribution. They are seen as adjuncts to a training course and promote the image of a trainer rather than a consultant. In fact a lot more than image is at stake if the consultant does not give due weight to the pre-implementation stages of consultancy, for symptoms are distinguished from causes during these stages, underlying problems are identified, tailored interventions are designed and client involvement and commitment are cemented. These are the areas where the consultant's contribution is most valuable and should be charged for. The shift of emphasis probably comprises the single most important change of attitude that helps trainers make the transition to consultancy.

Reduced fees There may be occasions when consultants agree to a reduced fee because they particularly want to be involved in a project as a result of personal conviction or seeing it as offering them a unique development opportunity. In order to maintain the effectiveness of contracting it is important that such an agreement is made openly and honestly.

Consultants who allow themselves to be jockeyed into accepting a reduced fee can easily resent this later and consciously or unconsciously give less than their best. Even if this does not happen, they may be overloading themselves, making up the lost fees by taking on extra work elsewhere, and thereby reducing their effectiveness.

In addition, offering a low fee as a way of getting work in the early days can be a trap that corners a consultant into being seen as cut-rate. It is difficult to increase rates after gaining entry without the risk of the client feeling cornered; and it is futile secretly to underestimate the time needed for a project, when a vicious circle is thus created in which future realistic estimates are seen as inflated. The important thing is for consultants to be honest with their clients and themselves.

Encouraging client involvement

A collaborative approach involves an attitude of mind and some explicitly negotiated agreements. Once this is achieved, consultants and clients can find many possibilities for joint work throughout a consulting contract. We outline below some of the possibilities, and Chapters 5, 7 and 9 contain examples of collaborative consultancy in practice:

- Decide together what information is needed, who has it and how to collect it; involve the client's resources in the actual collection.
- Summarize and present data to the client in a descriptive way, for joint analysis and diagnosis; invite those who supplied the data to extract the significance; offer interpretations and observations as suggestions only; focus on avoided areas and encourage debate.
- Engage in joint design work. Provide frameworks and ideas and invite the client's comments and additions; outline options and help clients choose; aim to achieve joint ownership of proposals; present ideas together to senior management or act as third parties in discussions between interested groups.
- During implementation, neither leave clients completely

unsupported nor 'do it for them'; if running a development event is involved, ask clients to attend or, co-work with them on different aspects of the programme.
- Review progress together regularly.
- At the end of the project, discuss lessons learnt and future directions for both parties.

A collaborative relationship once established cannot then be taken for granted, but requires regular attention. One can easily become immersed in the detail of the tasks and lose sight of the process. Some possible indications that all is not well include:
- Clients becoming repeatedly 'unavailable'.
- Insuffient time being allocated for meetings.
- Consultants being steered towards client contacts without the authority to make decisions.
- Clients wanting more and more detail.
- The consultant's credentials being questioned.
- Clients suddenly becoming compliant, agreeing with everything the consultant says.

Signals such as these indicate that mutual trust is faltering. It takes courage not to accept them at face value, but to find opportunities to state in a clear, non-threatening and non-defensive way what the consultant is experiencing, so that concerns can be openly discussed and resolved rather than avoided.

In this chapter we have described the nature of the development path for those moving from training to consulting. The challenge for many trainers is acquiring skills in building and maintaining collaborative relationships with clients. The next chapter provides one example of what this can mean in practice.

Notes

1. Block, P. *op. cit.*
2. Bennett, R. *op cit.*
3. Freedman, A.M. 'Client/Consultant Contact Problems', in Lee R.J. and Freedman A.M. (eds) *CONSULTATION SKILLS READING*, NTL Institute 1984.

5　The Training Consultant

This chapter has three sections. Firstly, we consider ways of gaining entry, since this is often a worry for those just starting to move into consultancy. Secondly, there is a description of a consulting assignment carried out by an internal consultant. Thirdly, we compare internal and external consultant roles and outline their probable strengths and weaknesses.

Ways of gaining entry

Training consultants with established reputations can expect potential clients to seek their services at least some of the time. In the transition period trainers are often more concerned with gaining access to managers through their own initiative. Here are some ideas for gaining entry, starting with approaches which are most readily available to trainers and progressing to those which become more appropriate as experience increases:

1. Follow-up meetings with selected course members.
2. Widening the scope of a training needs survey.
3. Special projects requiring research with managers.
4. Mounting a special event to spark interest in consultancy.
5. Self-education visits.
6. Using insider knowledge to target potential clients.
7. Joint publishing (with clients) in in-house journals.

Post-course follow-up

The debriefing of participants after a course is often the responsibility of the nominating manager unless some form of follow-up and evaluation has been planned as part of the training. Many trainers are prevented from doing as much follow-up with course members as they would like, because of the demands that regular direct training makes on their time.

The post-course meeting is an obvious consultancy opportunity and for this purpose it is easier to be selective about which people to arrange to see. For example:

- Those participants with whom the trainer has already established a relationship of mutual respect and who are clearly keen to apply and develop further the course material.
- Those participants in a position to sponsor the development of others and have the power to make decisions.
- Those from a team or department who are nominating significant numbers for a training programme. Perhaps a tailored version would be a more efficient and effective use of resources.
- Those from a part of the organization notable for *not* nominating many people for training courses (a rare chance to gain entry perhaps).

It is a relatively simple matter for trainers to start viewing course members as potential clients and to arrange follow-up meetings during a programme. A three-way meeting to include the participant's boss is a useful way of gaining entry to a higher level in the organization. A review of the application of course learning gives the trainer the opportunity to open the discussion to wider development issues in the manager's area of responsibility.

Widening the scope of a training needs survey

Trainers usually design data collection to uncover generalized training needs, they may thereby also acquire useful information on where there may be opportunities for consultancy. We also know several training departments that launched themselves into consulting work by giving managers the opportunity to request it. Rather than asking about training needs, they conducted surveys that invited managers to describe what services they needed to manage development in the organization. As we noted in Chapter 1, many managers' requirements can be better met by internal consultancy than standard training courses, and responses to the survey reflected this. This strategy implies that the training department is willing to encourage possible criticism and complaint from its customers, in order to fuel and support change.

Taking on special projects

Any project that gives a trainer a legitimate reason for arranging meetings with key managers throughout the organization is an opportunity to gain entry. We spoke to several trainers whose internal consultancy careers began in this way. One researched proposals for setting up the training and development function as a business centre, another undertook the revision of forms used for appraisal purposes, and another looked at the successes and difficulties faced by groups of participants on training courses who resolved to continue meeting after courses in order to promote mutual development. All became adept at widening the discussion from their initial entry point in order to uncover possible consulting opportunities.

Mounting a special event

Organizing one-off 'management briefings' on a topic of current organizational concern was the method one group of trainers used to initiate dialogue with managers and stimulate interest in further collaboration. Themes included:

- 'Stress at work – how do we identify and manage it?'
- 'Do we need more entrepreneurs?'
- 'Vision-building: how is it different from strategic planning?'
- 'Corporate culture: let's look at ours.'

The trainers' aim was to introduce potential clients to new ideas in ways that invited joint exploration of their usefulness and relevance for current management concerns. This approach lends itself to a fruitful collaboration between internal and external consultants. The external provides a focus, bringing in particular knowledge and experience. Externals are sometimes given a hearing where internal people are not, and they have the opportunity to ask important, naive or difficult questions. The internal consultant can provide an in-company point of view on the material, brief the external consultant on what issues to focus on and build interest and contacts. The collaboration is usually more productive than either party working independently.

The more such events can become a forum for discussion rather than just presentation, the greater the opportunity for contact with managers on the basis of joint problem identification. A variety of formats, such as working lunches, breakfasts, or an after-hours colloquium, as well as a half or 1-day seminar, all offer the chance of gaining entry and building consultant–client rather trainer–trainee relationships. The 'swap-shop' meetings held by the Association for Management Education and Development[1] are organized along these lines.

Doing this well means keeping up to date with current issues in the organization and linking these with professional knowledge and contacts in a wider field. This sort of homework is essential anyway for building competence and credibility as a consultant.

Self-education visits

The need to keep informed of organizational issues and trends is a continuing necessity in consulting. Peters and Austin[2] have popularized the strategy of MBWA (Managing by Walking About). The similar strategy of LBWA (Learning by Walking About) is one that consultants can use for the dual purpose of self-education and gaining entry. We have found that as long as consultants do not pick the week before the budget has to be submitted or another equally fraught time, then managers are very willing to talk about their own experience, ideas and concerns. A visit on this basis is more welcome than a sales call as long as it is genuine. Managers can become understandably resentful when an educational visit suddenly turns into a hard sell. Listening attentively, asking good questions, demonstrating understanding and offering some fresh thoughts and ideas in exchange, are forms of behaviour more likely to impress a potential client than any amount of persuasive sales talk.

Although this approach sows seeds for the future rather than producing immediate results, a proportion of such visits are likely to lead eventually to consulting assignments. For the less experienced consultant, this is also an opportunity to practise consulting skills with minimal risk. The starting point can be anything from the straightforward 'I would like to understand more about the work of your department and the particular challenges facing you as its manager', to something more specific, such as 'I'm interested in your views about the impact new technology has made in your department' or 'I'm writing an article on the Manager as Developer and I would like to discuss some of the points with you'.

Using insider knowledge

One internal consultant said he used his knowledge of the company to identify 'pain points' in the organization where managers were under pressure owing to planned reorganization, high turnover, expansion, the introduction of new systems, or poor morale. He would approach those he saw to be 'in pain' and ready for change with an offer to explore with them ways in which he could offer consulting help. He gained his information through an informal network of contacts and by scanning records and plans. He gained entry by making an appearance in times of difficulty and acquiring a reputation as a valuable resource to a trouble-shooting team. Another consultant we spoke to said her tactic was to identify people moving into new positions in the organization. She would time a visit at the point when they might be most open to changing things and interested in initiating new ventures.

Publishing

Once consulting projects are in progress, it is possible to publicize them by writing up the work in an in-house journal. Co-authoring with a client manager, describing honestly both the successes and the learning from whatever difficulties arose, is a way of ensuring that the piece excites the interests of other managers. Here the consultant is writing for potential clients rather than professional colleagues.

Points for external consultants

Most of what we have written above applies to the internal consultant. Consultants who are not selling packaged approaches which can be marketed tend to rely on building a reputation that will encourage new clients to contact them. Most use some or all of the following:

- Attending/presenting at national and international professional conferences.
- Publishing in journals/writing books.
- Mounting a few open programmes to give people a 'taste' of their work.
- Forming peer networks, where colleagues offer each other entry opportunities.
- Becoming associates of institutes or university departments which offer consultancy services.
- Becoming members of professional bodies that act as referral agencies for consultants or furnish potential clients with lists of accredited members.

A training consultancy assignment

As a way of illustrating in more detail the work of the training consultant there follow some extracts from a report written by an internal consultant, whom we shall call Alison Wright. We met as a result of carrying out a team-building and consultancy skills programme for the training group to which she belonged. Originally she had written some notes solely for her own use but then agreed to expand them for inclusion in this book. Her organization was a large insurance company and her department (T & D) had recently become a profit centre. Names have been changed to preserve confidentiality.

Background to the assignment

I had run quite a number of assertiveness programmes for my company but these had all been on an 'open' basis. When David Franklin, the personnel manager, rang me to discuss a special course for the new graduate intake, I was pleased, but a little nervous. I was not used to negotiating about costs and I did not know David that well, although I had met some of his staff on courses.

The entry interview

I went to David's office and he quickly said that he had heard good things about me and my courses. He had seen the programme description and objectives for an assertiveness skills course and he was sure it was just right for the particular group he had in mind. The reason for the training, he said, was that the graduates (average age 25) were technically highly competent, but many of them failed to make contributions at meetings, allowed themselves to be talked down, and generally seemed slow to take initiatives. They were all coming to the end of their year-long probationary period, known as the Graduate Development Programme, and it was intended that the course would help them to be successful in moving on to a permanent appointment.

In response I had a strong inclination simply to say yes, particularly since T & D had been wanting to build bridges with the personnel department for some time and I wanted to be seen as helpful. However, just as I was reminding myself not to take everything at face value, David made the additional comment that he would want reports on each of the participants. Their performance on the course would form part of the final assessment of the probationary period. I replied that reports were not normally made on course participants and that I believed it was only through a strict rule of confidentiality that people would be sufficiently open about themselves and each other that they could acquire assertiveness skills.

After some further probing I discovered that his real concern was with one individual, Paul, a borderline case who might fail the probationary period because of his quietness. Eventually David agreed that it did not make sense to jeopardize the programme and that an informal follow-up with Paul would be the best way of approaching the problem. So, in addition to the follow-up work which I would undertake, David would see each person individually.

The discussion about Paul led me to be rather more cautious and I decided that it really would be important for me to do some preliminary work, meet each of the intended participants and find out more about their training needs. There was another reason for this. One of my colleagues was having difficulty in another part of the organization because not enough attention had been paid to preliminary work. A group of managers had been brought together to attend a course on managing change. They were responsible for various local offices where a lot of new technology was being introduced. The course had been halted after half a day because the group were furious about the lack of support they were getting, in particular delays in the installation of new equipment. I did not want to find myself in such a position because I had not investigated the context for the training.

David was surprised about my insistence on the need for preliminary work but I felt that I would rather risk losing the assignment than get into the same mess as my colleague. I held my ground, explaining my reasons and we reached agreement on some preliminary interviews.

The working contract

I felt generally happy about how the discussions had gone. However, I did not feel that I had achieved a fully collaborative relationship. It was as if I was being employed, rather than we were jointly seeking to solve a problem. Having talked to one of my colleagues, I decided that I could perhaps change the relationship a little by getting David involved in decisions about the data collection. I included this in my letter to him:

Dear David,

I am writing to confirm our agreements of last Thursday when we discussed the running of an assertiveness programme for last year's graduate intake. The objectives for this programme would be that they:

- Acquire an increased sense of self-confidence.
- Become more willing to express their views to senior managers.
- Contribute more fully to the interdisciplinary project teams to which they belong.

The programme will be highly participative, based on real work problems, with plenty of opportunity for skill development.

We agreed that a total of 3 days' preliminary work would be necessary:

- One and a half days of interviews, to identify the participants particular training needs.
- One and a half days to analyse the data and finalize the course design.

When I have gathered my thoughts for the interview I would like to check with you to see if you have any additions or comments. I would also like you to brief the graduates about the proposed programme before the interviews.

We agreed that the course would be residential, probably lasting 3 days, to be followed by a 1-day meeting with the group to review their progress.

I will maintain confidentiality about individuals, although I will let you know in general terms whether I felt the objectives were met.

The only unknown which concerns me at this stage is that the data collected from the participants may lead us to reconsider the focus or emphasis of the training. At this stage the estimate of my time for this project is 7 days at the fee rate we discussed, namely £---- per day.

I shall ring you next week to check any queries or concerns you might have.

Yours sincerely,

ALISON WRIGHT

Data collection

A week later I had confirmation that I could go ahead to the next stage. At our next brief meeting I tried to raise with David the questions that should be put to the graduates during the interviews, but he was not interested and I decided to let the matter drop. He seemed to think I should know what to ask and he did not have much time to talk then. I decided that, when interviewing the graduates, I would give an explanation of why the course was being proposed, a rough outline of the content and then ask them:

- 'Do you think you have needs in this area?'
- 'Are there any particular problems you have encountered?'
- 'What do you think of the proposed course?'
- 'Do you have any suggestions about other areas which might usefully be covered?'

I also wanted to gather some additional information about how they were feeling about their training generally and any other factors which might influence their attitude to the course.

Having carried out the interviews, I found the important data which emerged were:

- Several were suspicious about the proposed training, believing it masked an adverse judgement which had not been communicated directly.
- Most of them agreed that they did want help in being more assertive (in some instances this was confirmed by how they actually behaved during the interview).
- There was widespread dissatisfaction about the Graduate Development Programme. They felt that either they were being thrown in the deep end, with too much being expected of them too soon, or else they were put in 'non-jobs' where they were bored.
- Most of the group felt under considerable stress.
- Four members of the group shared a flat and spent a lot of social time together.

With these data in mind I had a number of concerns:

- Those that were living together might be unwilling to give each other honest feedback; or alternatively they might bring too many domestic issues to the course.
- Assertiveness might be too narrow a focus, bearing in mind the other needs they had expressed.
- The course might become a dumping ground for bad feelings about the organization. Like the managers on the change course, they might be so resentful that they would be unwilling to look at how they themselves might improve.

I was also beginning to have doubts about whether one trainer would be enough, and I was regretting not having mentioned at any stage the possibility that two trainers might be needed. Maybe I had let possessiveness about the project get in the way of good sense.

Some of these concerns I was able to resolve in my own mind. Regarding the close personal relationships it seemed to me that this issue could be raised at the beginning of the course and that agreement could probably be reached between us on the best way to manage this. The course content also did not appear to be an insuperable obstacle; it would be relatively easy to redesign so that other organizational skills, e.g. stress management and time management, could be included as well as assertiveness.

However, the question of the graduates' resentment about their training in general was something I needed to discuss with David.

The proposal

I did not want to go into print with my concerns, even though David was expecting a written report. I knew that the matter of graduate recruitment was a source of some intense debate in the personnel department. I did not want any document that I might produce to be used for fighting a minor political battle, especially one where I was unsure about David's position.

I raised these points with him when we met. His first reaction was one of surprise at the degree of resentment; but then we both decided that since assertiveness was one of the training needs, it was perhaps not surprising that they had restricted expression of their feelings to moaning sessions with each other; perhaps anyway they were afraid that any expression of dissatisfaction would be held against them in the final assessment. It also revealed a lack of consistent monitoring and feedback to the graduates about their progress. David seized on this eagerly, as it clearly confirmed one of his own concerns about the way the Graduate Development Programme was operating.

We achieved common ground and indeed a more collaborative relationship when we both recognized that some genuine training needs should not be sacrificed for the sake of fuelling a political debate that was highly unlikely to be resolved for some time to come. We agreed that we should raise and deal with the graduates' feelings about their induction in a way that was integrated into the design of the course.

David was much less accommodating when I said that maybe I would need an additional trainer to help me. He was loath to pay the extra money and felt that with my experience of running assertiveness courses I should have known what the proper resourcing was likely to be.

After some discussion we linked the two problems and came up with a single solution. David agreed that he would work with me for part of the course. In this way he would be able to get some direct feedback about the Graduate Development Programme; also the participants would have the chance to practise their assertiveness skills.

With this issue dealt with there was little disagreement over extending the length of the course to include a wider range of topics.

This meeting had turned out to be the most difficult part of the whole assignment, but I was now in a position to put forward a formal written proposal:

Dear David,
As agreed at our last meeting I enclose the objectives and outline design for the training programme.

The main change from our initial thinking is the inclusion of a session when you will visit the group to discuss the Graduate Development Programme. I think that this may provide some useful information on which you can build, and the participants themselves will be able to practise their assertion skills; I shall do my best to discourage a 'dumping session', although I think that inevitably it will be partly such. My suggestion is that you send each person a briefing letter about the programme, explaining the purpose of your session so they can gather their thoughts. I shall ring you soon to discuss this further.

A follow-up day will take place about a month after the course, when progress on the action plans will be reviewed. Our hope is that you will be able to attend that day, but we agreed to make a final decision nearer the time.

I should also like to confirm that another 2 days of my time is required because of the course being lengthened and some additional design work being required.

I feel that we have found a good way of handling some potentially difficult areas and believe that the course stands every chance of being successful.

Yours sincerely,

ALISON WRIGHT

Implementation and follow-up

The course went well, although the session when David came down was difficult for me to handle. In particular I sometimes needed to be an intermediary, focusing everybody on the quality of their communication and ensuring that key points were logged. The review of the session from the perspective of people's assertion skills was very helpful.

The follow-up in this assignment consisted of more than the follow-up day itself. I arranged a meeting with David some 3 months after the course. In considering the project as a whole, we were pleased with the outcomes and that we had been able to insulate the training from the organizational politics. David expressed appreciation that I had insisted on the preliminary work, although he had had doubts about it at the time. There was no immediate possibility of further work together, so we both saw this as a suitable point for closure.

Commentary

In reviewing the project with us, Alison was generally pleased. She felt that she had been successful in a number of ways:

- Probing beyond the client's initial statements, e.g. uncovering the real reason why David wanted reports on the participants.
- Undertaking some preliminary data collection rather than offering an immediate packaged solution to the client's first perception of the problem. We pointed out to her that she had still found it difficult to let go of course design until *after* she had investigated the target group's training needs. Her interviews were centred on an outline programme she had already prepared, thus guiding everyone's thinking in the same direction. She agreed that she had found it difficult to approach the interviews with an open, curious mind and had taken the course design with her as a prop.
- Building a collaborative relationship with her client. Alison felt that she had achieved this by continually discussing and resolving with David the issues raised by the programme. By engaging in joint problem-solving, her sense of being 'under instructions' had dissolved. She recognized that each time she had faced and talked through a potentially difficult area it had taken some courage on her part but had always proved rewarding. She agreed that it was important to aim for collaboration when it really mattered rather than use it as a technique. For example, trying to involve David in formulating interview questions, in this case, was inappropriate, in contrast to her proposal that he should work with her on the course when the graduates were invited to air their views of the induction programme.
- Checking agreements made. Alison said that writing to David about her understanding of their discussions had been an important discipline and had helped her to shape the progress of the assignment.
- Renegotiating her contract. Alison realized that initially she had been overly keen to prove herself and to be able to claim sole credit for any success in handling the assignment. She felt that she needed to be more willing to ask for help from

her colleagues. She would then have considered earlier the possibility of needing two trainers to resource the programme. She was, however, very pleased that she had been assertive in renegotiating with David about this.

Internal v external consultancy

One of the points that arose from our review discussion with Alison was the difference between the position of internal consultants, who are a part of the total client system, and external consultants, who clearly are not.[3] Alison felt that operating as a profit-centre increased her sense of independence, but that she had become aware, even on this first consulting assignment, of how much she felt constrained by the organizational politics. This led us to compare the advantages and disadvantages of internal and external consultants.

The internal consultant

ADVANTAGES
* Knows the system (formally and informally) and how to use it.
* Knows the language and how to express ideas in an accepted way.
* May know the key people and how to influence them.
* May have a well established network of contacts.
* May already have a lot of information about the problem.
* Can work unobtrusively at times.
* Is well placed to seize opportunities.
* Is less likely to be expected to provide instant solutions than the external consultant.
* Can keep in close touch with the longer-term consequences of a project.

DISADVANTAGES
* May have difficulty establishing credibility and indeed visibility.
* Has a history which may get in the way – past failures, old allegiances.

- May be too much part of the system – not sufficiently detached. Indeed may be part of the problem.
- May be *seen* to be too much part of the system, thus limiting trust.
- May feel wary of confronting, especially senior managers.
- May be subject to political/hierarchical pressures.
- May have limited room for manoeuvre because of tight role definitions.
- May not be able to refuse projects.

The external consultant

ADVANTAGES
- Is more likely to be seen as outside the politics of the organization.
- People are more likely to be open.
- People may be more willing to listen to and hear this 'outsider'.
- Can bring new perspectives and fresh insights.
- Can more easily provide contacts with other organizations.
- Can become an important communication channel, especially upwards.
- Likely to have high visibility because of people's heightened expectations.
- Can more easily be direct and confronting.
- Has freedom to turn down an assignment.

DISADVANTAGES
- May be 'put on a pedestal', leading to deference/resentment/disillusionment.
- May need a lot of time to discover how the system *really* works.
- May only see part of the problem.
- Leaves at the end of a project and may not see the longer-term results.
- May use ideas which are too different from the organization's current way of thinking.

In assessing these lists we reached two conclusions. Firstly, we recognized that internal and external consultants working together have the potential to be a highly effective partnership if they make conscious use of the benefits of each other's position and help each other overcome the drawbacks. Secondly, we came to believe that internal consultants were likely to be more effective if, as far as possible, they managed themselves and their client relationships as though they were external. In effect, they had to become aware 'outsiders' working on the inside. This role meant monitoring closely the use of their time and its cost-effectiveness; negotiating wants and offers, not only with clients, but with bosses and colleagues as well; assessing the validity and development nature of assignments; striving to occupy a position that was not too firmly fixed in the company's hierarchical structure, but allowed maximum freedom of access; and acquiring the discipline of regularly stepping back from organizational politics, and balancing political sense and independence of mind and action.

This chapter has illustrated the work of the training consultant by following Alison Wright's progress on a single assignment. It is interesting that as soon as she became involved in designing a training intervention for a client manager she came closer to having to deal with 'live' organizational issues rather than stay with the relatively safer simulations of general training courses. It was noticeable that she felt far less comfortable handling the session on the course when the graduates discussed the induction programme with the personnel manager. This called for Alison to act far more in the roles of facilitator, mediator or process consultant than trainer. In the next two chapters we discuss the further development someone like her would need to undertake.

Notes

1. The address of the Association of Management Education and Development is:
   Premier House,
   77 Oxford St.,
   London W1R 1RB Telephone 01 439 1188
2. Peters T. and Austin N. *A PASSION FOR EXCELLENCE*, Collins 1985.
3. For further reading on the differences between internal and external consultants see Swartz, D.H. 'Similarities and Differences of Internal and External Consultants', *JOURNAL OF EUROPEAN INDUSTRIAL TRAINING*, Vol. 4, No. 5, 1975.

6 From Training to Learning

Introduction

Some organizations find that the combination of general training courses and training consultancy provides the right mix of flexibility and continuity for their management development needs. Others are finding that this approach is not sufficient. Some are caught in a series of dilemmas that have forced a radical revision of their development activities, as is well illustrated by the problems facing the European management development manager of an expanding micro-chip technology company.

It is a well established pattern that after an initial period of growth and tremendous flexibility, organizations often settle into more closely defined structures and procedures as a way of controlling the extra complexities that sheer size has brought. There's a plateau period of consolidation. We believe as a company that our survival depends on us not doing this, on our ability to keep up the momentum of change and growth. We're facing enormous challenges. We need to keep recruiting an ever higher calibre of employee from an apparently shrinking pool of talent. We need our staff to be repeatedly changing their skill areas as we introduce new systems to manage the systems we already have. As we expand, we are also removing whole layers of management, merging functions and reshaping the organization so that peoples' roles and jobs are being constantly redefined. As a result, the demand for training is soaring. Responding to this at face value means we are engaging in a race we cannot win. We simply are unable to design and run training courses fast enough to meet the rate of change in people's development needs. Training is in danger of becoming a brake on our progress.

Compare this with the problems facing the head of trainer training at a very different kind of company, one of the clearing banks:

We are at an impasse at the moment as long as we keep on thinking in terms of running training courses in the traditional way, no matter how well designed. More and more demands are being placed on branches and areas to exercise greater responsibility for meeting targets in a more competitive market place and with tighter resources. The demand for staff development is therefore increasing just at a time when there is less willingness to release people for training.

These two examples illustrate the practical problems that force development specialists to question their operating assumptions and pursue fresh lines of enquiry:

- How can we develop people without sending them on training courses?
- How can we make training productive in terms of operational tasks?
- How can we share with managers more of the responsibility for training?
- How can we get people to train each other and themselves?
- How can we deal with different training needs simultaneously?

Organizations have been experimenting with a variety of methods which provide some solutions to these questions. These fall into five main categories which we will outline briefly.

Distance learning methods

These methods are experiments in bringing development to employees instead of the other way round. They are also ways of multiplying and distributing development resources which are far less costly than the specialized staff needed for face-to-face training. They include video, audio and computer packages, national broadcasts, programmed learning texts, reading material, computer networking and correspondence courses. In some companies the development function sees itself operating as a mini 'open college'.

Self-directed learning workshops

Where courses are still considered an important part of development activities, companies are dealing with a diverse set of development needs on the same programme by including designs in which course members work on their different learning goals by drawing on the resources available. We have heard this described as the 'play-school' approach, where a diversity of needs and resources are mixed and matched in creative ways in a joint undertaking between course leaders and course members.

Action learning sets

This widely used approach was developed originally by Reg Revans. Small groups of managers meet regularly as a 'set' with the help of a set adviser to work on the tasks and problems facing each member. Instead of running a number of courses with one group of course members after another, a set adviser may be working with many different sets, each of which may meet for maybe 1 day a month. In a sense 'courses' are thus scattered in space and time throughout the organization, dealing with the actual development needs of managers as they arise, with the set advisers helping to create and catalyse the conditions in which these problem-solving 'cells' can thrive.

Self-development groups

More loosely structured groups than action learning sets, they are less primarily task-focused, where members can identify, explore and work on their development needs. The boundaries of this exploration may be closely or widely defined. Work, domestic, practical, emotional, task and personal issues may be addressed. This approach is often seen as a seeding process on the part of the development function. The groups may be formed on courses as syndicate groups or 'support and challenge groups' that continue to meet after the programme. Development specialists may actively start a number of such groups by putting people in touch with one another and helping the groups to establish ways of working together which will enable them to become self-sustaining. These ideas are also informing some team-building approaches.

Developing managers as developers

Some organizations are giving this area priority for investing their development resources. The skill and expertise needed for developing people becomes one of the core competences for general line management, instead of residing in a separate specialist function. This function is then staffed not with developers, but with developers of developers whose tasks then become:

1. Designing ways of developing this new core competence. (Paradoxically this sometimes is seen as running a whole new breed of training courses for managers.)
2. Designing procedures and resources to support managers in their role as developers.

The nature of this development path

In Chapter 4 we discussed the development path from training to consulting in terms of new demands placed on trainers to learn how to develop collaborative relationships with client managers. We suggested that this required a qualitatively different way of working which trainers may not necessarily have acquired.

Although it might appear that trainers or training consultants could take on the new activities outlined above relatively easily, we have seen again and again that unless people understand their work in terms of learning rather than training, then the new activities are unsuccessful. Initiatives begun with optimism peter out. New approaches fail somehow to take hold in the organization. Distance learning packages are made widely available, but turn out to be scarcely used; the membership of action learning sets tails off; self-development group meetings degenerate into social events and then cease altogether; participants and leaders on self-directed learning workshops end up frustrated and dissatisfied, vaguely blaming one another for expectations that have not been met; managers attend courses on developing staff and then return to work and nominate their staff for other courses.

One common cause of these problems is that wider organizational issues are not being considered. We shall address this point when we look at the third development path in Chapter 8.

The second cause is that the development specialists responsible for initiating these projects have not developed a learning-based approach. They are doing learning-based activities with a training-based orientation and training-based skills and techniques. The change from developing people to enabling their self-development calls for a fundamental shift in values, aims and approach. To uncover these we shall now look at the principles underlying what is variously called self-motivated learning, self-directed learning or management self-development, and which we are referring to as learning-based approaches. These are:

1. People can only choose to learn; they cannot be made to learn.
2. All activities are opportunities for learning.
3. Different people learn in different ways.
4. People who have learned how to learn are the best equipped to deal with continuous change.

People can only choose to learn; they cannot be made to learn

To understand the significance of this principle we need to differentiate learning, as we use the term, from what is more aptly termed memorizing. People can memorize knowledge, behaviour and attitudes, storing for later use what others have taught or shown them. This capacity is very useful for rapid adaptation. A large amount of childhood socialization is acquired in this way and traditionally our education system has compounded this further.

Memorizing has particular characteristics. The material is swallowed whole, added to an individual's store and reproduced when the appropriate trigger is activated, either by conscious choice or unconsciously because of a stimulus in the environment. Neither the memorizer nor the material is fundamentally changed in the process, although the material may be distorted by the memorizer's own filter.

Learning is quite different. New material is assimilated by being thoroughly chewed and digested; then unwanted bits are rejected. The learner thus changes the material and is changed by it. This is the dynamic process of learning.

Going back to the principle we are discussing, it is possible to see how people can memorize things almost passively. But fully integrated learning requires of the learner a highly active, discriminating involvement.

Training courses are often geared more to memorizing than to learning. Trainees memorize concepts and information when they attend effective presentations with good visual aids. Training films reinforce the points in memorable ways, using graphics, humour or dramatic devices. Trainers design exercises for course members to practise and become familiar with certain skills and techniques; they may demonstrate and model behaviours for trainees to copy. The concern of many trainers is the decay over time of this kind of 'learning' and the need for immediate application and reinforcement at work.

Undoubtedly integrated learning also takes place on training courses; the more participative the training, the more opportunity there is for this to happen. However, most trainers and course members are comfortable and familiar with a balance of responsibility that is weighted towards the trainer. Course members may expect to work hard, but there is a tendency for all parties to underestimate how strong is the expectation that people will be told what to learn, how to learn and how successfully they have learned.

The most important aspect of this first principle, then, is the shift towards far greater learner responsibility for the development process. With a learning approach, the involvement of learners in every stage of the development process is not just desirable, but all important, because their motivation and commitment are paramount. Such an approach presents difficulties for trainers on the training to learning development path. It means that those treading it must:

- Review how truly self-responsible they are being for their own development. If they are avoiding this, they will certainly fail in their attempts to enable others to become more self-responsible.
- Learn to recognize the many ways in which others avoid or struggle with taking on greater self-responsibility.
- Learn to intervene helpfully at these points without taking back all the responsibility.

These needs turn out to be just the tip of the iceberg. Those pursuing this path find themselves grappling with many difficult questions that force them to reappraise their values and sense of purpose. Consider the following:

- If I accept that individuals should identify their own development needs, do I accept all those needs as valid in the business context? If not, on what basis do I make the distinction? Is it up to me to make the distinction?
- How much do I believe I know what is best for people? How much of my self-esteem is tied up with people wanting to be dependent on my help? What sort of help should I be giving? What is 'help'?
- If I see people not facing up to their responsibilities, is it because they do not want to or because they do not understand what this means? What is my responsibility in this?
- If people put pressure on me to teach them the 'right' answers, how do I respond? What are the consequences?

What distinguishes training specialists from learning specialists is their willingness to struggle with these complex issues, without paralyzing themselves, even though such questions can never be finally resolved.

All activities are opportunities for learning

Alan Mumford[1] has referred to 'informal managerial development' as the haphazard process whereby managers learn as they are promoted, change jobs, handle crises and work with different people. Management development specialists have traditionally sought to organize this otherwise chance process by succession planning, secondments and special projects. The idea is to give managers opportunities to acquire certain experience and skills at particular times in their careers, in a way that benefits both the individuals and the organization. This approach to management development seeks to control and manage learning opportunities as instruments for meeting anticipated business requirements. The emphasis is on the end result of the learning, the new knowledge and skills which managers can bring to their work. In this sense, the learning process itself is merely the vehicle for improved task achievement.

The shift in perception inherent in a learning-based approach is threefold. Firstly, there needs to be a recognition that *all* organizational tasks can be a source of conscious, self-directed learning by managers. Secondly comes the ability to set learning goals *and* task achievement goals for all activities. Thirdly, learning and task achievement become vitally interdependent, neither one merely the vehicle for the other.

The development need on the training to learning path is a considerable increase in creativity for:

- Recognizing developmental resources.
- Realizing the opportunities for learning inherent in situations.
- Designing task achievement/learning opportunities.
- Releasing the creative energy in others that will fuel self-motivated development.

People learn in different ways

We now have a substantial body of knowledge about the nature of adult learning. The work of David Kolb[2] has been influential in identifying four stages in the process of learning (Figure 6.1).

His research showed that it is rare for individuals to give equal

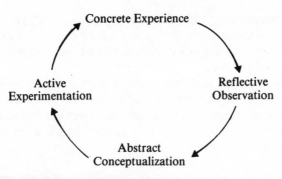

Figure 6.1   Kolb's learning cycle

emphasis to all four stages. People have learning preferences which determine the ease or difficulty with which they are able to learn from different kinds of experiences. Brain research has shown that people can organize information in different ways. Left-brain thinking is largely analytical and logical, right-brain thinking is more intuitive and holistic. People differ even in the way they take in information through their senses. Neuro-linguistic programming suggests that people are differentially attuned to visual, auditory and kinaesthetic stimuli.

Professionals interested in both training and learning draw on this information, but they tend to use it in different ways. A training approach which concentrates on the competences people acquire as the end result of training uses adult learning theory *implicitly* to design training courses to suit a range of learning preferences. The aim is to create situations in which people can acquire new knowledge and skills rapidly. A learning approach uses learning theory *explicitly* to help managers understand:

- How people learn.
- How learning can be blocked.
- Their own strengths and weaknesses as learners.
- How to create conditions for maximizing the strengths of their own learning style.
- How to build new strengths as learners and overcome blockages to learning in themselves and in the culture and structure of the organization.

Not only do people learn in different ways, what they learn will be unique to each individual. Training seeks to help people arrive at more or less the same end point whereas individual learning will be diverse and cannot be defined in advance in the same way as training objectives.

The development need along the training to learning path is to become thoroughly conversant with theories and models about the nature of adult learning and to be able to impart this understanding to managers in ways they can use for their own and others development.

People who have learned how to learn are better equipped to deal with continuous change

This principle provides the rationale for the learning approach in today's business world. In stable conditions organizations develop a set of operating norms which remain valid over time. To be successful, single-loop learning is sufficient. The term comes from cybernetics, the study of artificial intelligence, and describes a simple negative feedback system which enables self-regulation in steady state conditions. See Figure 6.2.

Double loop learning is required for self-regulation in turbulent times. It is so called because a second loop is drawn to represent the extra level of 'intelligence' needed to question the operating norms themselves. See Figure 6.3.

This difference is similar to that between 'learning' and 'learning to learn'. The latter mode requires people to challenge and change their goals and tasks as circumstances evolve by

Figure 6.2   Single loop learning

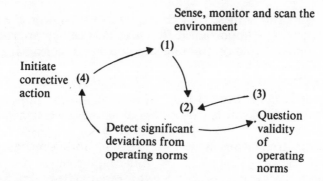

Figure 6.3   Double loop learning

recognizing and questioning the underlying assumptions on which these are based. This autonomous, flexible, proactive approach to managing at work is best matched by a learning-based approach to development which is more likely to foster exactly these qualities in people.

The development need for those seeking to use this approach in management development is to understand how to set up the conditions in which learning to learn can flourish. Gareth Morgan[3] suggests that this involves three key areas:

1. Acknowledging legitimate error as a source of learning of great practical value. Encouraging people to be open about and interested in mistakes and uncertainties.
2. Encouraging the exploration of difference and allowing constructive conflict and debate between competing perspectives. Encouraging the redefinition and reframing of problems instead of rushing straight into solutions.
3. Balancing people's need for structure and guidance with an appropriate level of autonomy and flexibility in the development process. Traditionally this has been achieved by defining fixed goals and objectives and allowing freedom in the choice of methods for achieving the desired outcomes. A deeper level of responsible autonomy is achieved by exploring and defining the constraints within which freedom of choice and action can be exercised. This means people identify for themselves goals *and* methods which are compatible with an agreed system of company values.

After elaborating these four principles, we are now in a position to extract some important differences between an approach to development based on training and one based on learning:

TRAINING	LEARNING
Training is an instrument for improving task achievement.	Learning is an all important goal, alongside task achievement.
Training often means memorizing the new.	Learning always means assimilating the new.
Trainees do not necessarily need to understand *how* they learn.	It is essential for learners to become aware of and actively manage their own learning.
Learning theory is used implicitly to design efficient training.	Learning theory is used explicitly to enable self-development.
Responsibility for training rests with the trainer. Trainee involvement in setting training objectives, choosing training methods and deciding how to evaluate them, is not essential.	Responsibility for learning rests with the learner. His/her involvement in all aspects of the development process is vital.
The desired outcomes of training are the same for all individuals.	The outcomes of learning are unique to each individual.
Prepares people for a known future.	Prepares people for an unknown future.

In this chapter we have tried to show that trainers cannot be expected to adopt learning-based approaches to development overnight. In order to become competent in this field they need above all to engage in their own self-development. Inevitably this will be a different route for every individual trainer but those who would like some practical ideas for getting started will find a self-development plan in Appendix 1 and should also refer to Suggested Reading.

In the next chapter we look at the work of learning consultants, who combine competences gained from two development paths, that of training to consulting and training to learning. The two paths are mutually reinforcing in many ways, so that experience gained in one is helpful for the other. For example, consulting experience requires good contracting skills, which are needed for negotiating learning contracts with managers. Similarly the interdependence of development goals and business goals in learning-based approaches makes for practical and productive consultancy.

Notes

1. Mumford A. 'Using Reality in Management Development', *MANAGE-MENT EDUCATION AND DEVELOPMENT*, Vol. 18, No. 3 1987.
2. Kolb D.A., Rubin, I.M. and McIntyre, J.M. *ORGANIZATIONAL PSY-CHOLOGY – AN EXPERIENTIAL APPROACH*, Prentice-Hall 1974.
3. Morgan G. *IMAGES OF ORGANIZATION*, Sage 1986.

7   The Learning Consultant

In the previous chapter we quoted a training manager concerned about the way that his organization handled the development of people. He believed that the members of his training team had too much of a course mentality; he wanted them to see their role in much wider terms. He talked about them becoming developers rather than trainers; using the nomenclature we have introduced in this book, it became clear that he wanted them to operate more as learning consultants. This chapter describes our work with that team.

A learning consultancy assignment

Early stages of the project

The team's current approach matched the expectations of participants and the generally bureaucratic nature of the organization, but it was not developmental. Managers and staff took very little responsibility for themselves, reinforcing a culture that was inimical to success in the newly competitive environment of the financial world. There was not as yet a climate in which self-motivated learning (our client's term) could flourish.

We needed to stimulate the team's thinking about their manager's vision of a radically different way of working. Since it was some time before the total group could meet, we recorded our initial discussion about the desired future on videotape, distributed it to the team members and asked them to respond in whatever way they wanted.

We learned a lot from this mistake. As individuals watched the video on their own, they were nonplussed and fearful of new and apparently enormous demands suddenly being placed on them. They had not contributed to the formulation of the vision and, far from being inspired, they were appalled, and responded in ways characteristic of the organization's culture. There was no outspoken rejection but a series of passively resistant ploys: silence, procrastination, evasion, bland comments, dutiful noises and a series of 'yes, but . . .' responses.

We realized that we had made a leap too far ahead of our clients' starting point. We had not set up the conditions for change in terms of the 'Gleicher formula',[1] which states that for change to occur $A \times B \times C > D$ where A is dissatisfaction with the present, B is desire for a new situation, C is awareness of the first practical steps and D is the cost of change, emotional as well as practical and financial. At this stage the team were simply counting the cost to themselves of adopting a very different way of working.

At this point we returned to a more structured approach in formulating our proposals for a working contract:

- To increase A (dissatisfaction with the present) we decided to encourage debate about the effectiveness of the current training approach in the light of the organization's future needs. We distributed reading materials and questions that would develop a wider perspective and curiosity from the team about the trends of change and their particular implications for training and development in the organization.
- To develop B (desire for a new situation) we offered a variety of ways that we could work with the team in their transition that would help them to experience, understand and we hoped, become excited by different approaches to development (see Figure 7.1).
- To clarify C (awareness of first steps) we needed to identify possible interim stages that the team could move through in developing towards learning consultant roles (see Figure 7.2).

1. **Team-building:** helping the team as a whole to develop.
2. **Joint Research:** to identify development needs within the organization and to assess the impact of new and existing training and development interventions.
3. **Design workshops:** helping the team members develop an innovative approach in designing new programmes and revitalizing existing ones.
4. **Co-leading:** on new programmes or activities where internal expertise is being developed or on external programmes arranged by the consultants.
5. **Development contracts:** through intensive small group tutorials and practice sessions or on a distance learning basis through audio and video tape.
6. **Counselling:** on an ad hoc basis or as part of a series of personal development sessions.
7. **Resource link:** providing information and advice on training and development activities and arranging contacts with other organizations.
8. **Co-consulting:** helping trainers make the transition towards a consultancy role within their own organization.

Figure 7.1   Options for using the external consultants

Developing a working contract

Our proposal suggested three phases for what became known as the Joint Development Project:
1. Interviews with team members, followed by some guided reading and exchange of comments by audio tape. At this point members would be asked if they were willing to make a provisional commitment to the project. On that basis they would then engage in an initial stock-take of their current knowledge and skills and begin identifying development needs. They would design this activity themselves calling on us as resources as necessary.
2. A workshop for all members of the team and their manager. The purpose of this event would be to
   (a) Review the current work of the team and team relationships.
   (b) Clarify roles and expectations regarding the Joint Development Project, including issues of resourcing and support.
   (c) Review the findings of the self and peer assessment and its implications for individual and team development
   (d) Test commitment to participating further in the project.

PRESENT TRAINERS	INTERIM STAGES			FUTURE DEVELOPERS
1	2	3	4	5
Runs standard courses in standard ways, to meet generalized training needs. Expects participants to reach the same end point. Takes responsibility for what happens on programmes and evaluates outcomes. Is mainly concerned with content.	Offers options within standard courses which allow participants to meet particular needs which arise within the programme aims. Helps people identify individual needs and select learning methods. Co-ordinates activities. Higher process concern.	Offers programmes within which there is considerable time for self-directed activities. Pre-course work with participants identifies needs and prepares for the course. Accepts that outcomes may vary widely within the aims of the programme. Helps people learn about learning and self-management.	Programme is jointly designed by total group when it comes together, after extensive pre-work. Everybody shares expertise and resources. 'Developer' manages the boundary and affirms the values and methods of self-managed learning and mutual development. Undertakes extensive follow-up. High level of process and task concern.	Negotiates long-term development contracts with individuals and groups. People engage in a variety of learning activities separately and together. Goals are continuously renewed and extended. Wide variety of roles including teacher, coach, mentor, counsellor, resource investigator, process consultant.

Figure 7.2 Learning consultant roles

3. Implementation of the development plans. Each member would have an agreed number of consultant days to draw on in assisting her or his development. They could join forces where needs were shared so as to use less consultant time. The principle was that they would be responsible for deciding when and how to use us as resources, to be as creative as possible in making the best use of us and to stretch us as much as we would aim to stretch them.

We identified a number of necessary conditions for the success of the Project. These were:

- A clear understanding of the values, rationale and practical implications of self-motivated learning.
- A willingness by all to help each member of the team identify specific developmental goals, together with means of measuring progress towards them.
- A shared commitment to offer support and challenge.
- Clarity about how much freedom each person really had in moving towards their developmental goals. Open discussion and negotiation about this.
- A willingness to try out different methods of learning.
- A willingness to bring back learning to the team and to build on one another's work.
- A willingness for each person only to make agreements they were really committed to.

This proposal was accepted by the team. In effect we had negotiated the kind of long-term development contract with them that they would themselves be setting up in future with their own internal clients.

Review of implementation

We went ahead with phases one and two of the proposal and then held a review with our client, the training manager. We felt that so far our design had been basically sound. We had modelled learning consultancy rather than training in a number of ways:

- During the workshop we gave no formal theory inputs, but simple models and ideas arising from phase (1) work were posted round the room at the outset as resources for all of us.

- A variety of books and other learning materials were available for participants to use whenever they wished.
- We regularly discussed and renegotiated our role with the group.
- We used the changes in our relationship with the group as a way of illustrating different training and consultant roles.
- We worked explicitly at the levels of task, procedures and process.
- We worked with the group's external boundaries (its new relationships with the rest of the organization), and its internal boundaries (the working relationships between team members and with the manager).

We were not satisfied at this point that we had resolved one difficult aspect of the group, which was indicative of the organization's culture as a whole – the tendency already mentioned for people to go along with things on the surface but then passively to sabotage by losing momentum. People were immensely skilful at providing the required response in a situation (including the apparent acceptance of self-responsibility!). They were accustomed to a basically dependent relationship with anyone they perceived to be in authority and our engagement by their manager as consultants was sufficient for us to be seen in such a role. They were keen and constructive in public, and floundered when left to continue working independently. Despite much discussion and negotiation (in hindsight a futile tactic), we knew the team remained dependent on external motivation. This block was right at the heart of any development towards a learning consultancy approach by the team.

We had also learned by this stage that the team members did not have a great deal of insight into their own behaviour and feelings. They lacked information about ways in which they could impede their own development or that of others, having had little exposure to any form of personal, as opposed to professional, development. They had found the process of self- and peer-assessment difficult to design or engage in, so that their initial learning goals were vague and relatively superficial. It was clear that they lacked the process skills so necessary for consultancy such as:

- Highly tuned listening and observation skills for picking up

the process level in group interaction or individual communication.
- Making 'here and now' interventions that worked explicitly
  or implicitly with the process level.
- Timing interventions, judging when to speak or act and when
  to remain silent.
- The capacity to give simple, direct feedback.

We believed that confronting the self-responsibility issues head
on would be counter-productive. We decided we needed to
redesign the next stages in order to:

- Provide opportunities for personal development.
- Transfer the tendency to meet others' expectations from the
  context of authority relationships (real or perceived) to a peer
  level.
- Remove individuals from the over-comfortable cohesiveness
  that seemed to take over when the team was working
  together.
- Provide sufficient support for individuals to feel more
  inclined to explore the areas of freedom open to them, rather
  than huddle defensively together in the centre of the field of
  play.

Redesign of the project

As a result of the review we agreed some structures in which the
further identification and implementation of individual and
team development plans could take place. A system of mentoring
and a self- and mutual-development group were created.

The mentoring was based on a contract between pairs within
the team and one external consultant. The three worked closely
together, and within this safer and yet challenging relationship
the danger of compliance was reduced. We realize that we have
rather distorted the definition of organizational mentor, which
usually refers to an older manager taking a younger manager
under his or her wing and offering both practical and emotional
help: encouragement in undertaking new assignments, role
modelling, sponsorship, counselling and friendship. Clearly this
can only take place when both parties belong to the same

organization; however, we felt that the word mentor still best described the flavour of the relationship.

The development group was directly related to the mentoring. It was made up of all members of the team, plus one of the mentors as facilitator at each meeting. The group provided a setting for:

1. Discussion of the progress individuals were making.
2. Skill development.
3. Discussing various training and consultancy problems.
4. Giving and receiving feedback.
5. Reviewing learning about the nature of self-development and planning ways in which this could be transferred to the team's work with organizational clients.

One of the outcomes of this phase of the project was an improvement in the relationship between the training manager and his team. Although his vision and enthusiasm were appreciated he had been seen as inconsistent in his style, sometimes taking a low profile and relying on his staff to use their initiative, then suddenly getting 'cold feet' and intervening with numerous demands. The development group was able to start establishing its own boundaries, to the point of giving the manager some clear feedback on what was helpful and unhelpful about the ways he managed them. The mentoring and the time in the development group were important for building this sort of confidence and autonomy, bearing in mind the extent of deference in the organization.

Final review and closure

In reviewing the project as a whole the manager and the team were satisfied that they had made considerable progress towards working more as learning consultants. They now saw themselves as being in the third and fourth columns of Figure 7.2:

- The number of standard courses was substantially reduced in favour of consulting assignments.
- There were few isolated training events; most courses were supported by extensive pre- and post-course work.

- There was far greater responsibility being placed on the learner.
- A number of distance learning packages were prepared.
- The level of motivation in the team was higher.
- Other groups of trainers in the organization approached this team for help in taking more of a learning consultant approach to their work.

There were a number of other aspects which we felt worthy of note.

Despite the innovations mentioned above there were still a number of standard training courses to be run. The training manager was keen to avoid a sharp division between the trainers and the learning consultants, and established two groups, but without fixed membership. The learning consultant group was made up of people temporarily seconded from the training group; it had a leader who was responsible for overseeing all developmental projects, but who would also in time return to training. The importance of cross-fertilization between the two groups was regarded as vital. One way of doing this was the institution of a project book into which any member of the whole group could write suggestions for areas of the team's work which would benefit from a learning consultancy approach. The whole team would hold regular meetings to decide which projects should be taken on.

An important impetus for team growth was the need to educate client managers about the changing approach and to negotiate with other groups of trainers in the organization. In planning and implementing their strategy the team members were also acquiring some important consultancy skills. Having a newcomer join the team half way through the project proved to be invaluable; she was curious and intelligent. As an outsider she was able to ask lots of naive questions which caused people to rethink what they were doing. In order for her to be successfully inducted, members of the team had to explain to her their understanding of the project and how it was progressing. The training manager now sees movement into and out of the team as helping it to 'keep its cutting edge'; it is forced regularly to reappraise what it is doing and the values which underpin its work.

The training manager now believes, and we agree with him, that we should have pushed him earlier to be more open with his own boss about his plans. We should have stressed the necessity for him to collaborate with his boss and indeed other parts of the organization as the various changes became apparent. As consultants we had colluded with somebody who saw himself as going out on a limb, allowing a somewhat covert start to the project and risking exactly the isolation that our client feared.

What makes this project an example of learning consultancy is the way the contract was limited to the development of the individual trainers and the team as a whole. The scope of the assignment did not allow us to address more explicitly the wider organizational culture. This extension of the project would have taken us into the field of organization change consultancy which is the subject of the next two chapters.

Note

1. Sheane D. 'Organization Development in Action', *JOURNAL OF EUROPEAN AND INDUSTRIAL TRAINING*, Vol. 2, No. 8 1978.

8 From Individual Change to Organizational Change

The two development paths already described require trainers to increase their understanding of the nature of consulting relationships and of adult learning and self-development. The third path takes the nature of change as a perspective that encompasses both of these and goes further in two ways:

1. A need for increased breadth. The capacity to work with the change and development of larger systems: from a single individual to a work group, to a larger unit of interlinked groups, to a whole organization and to systems of organizations such as the subsidiaries in a multi-national company.
2. A need for increased depth. The capacity to meet this greater complexity with cognitive maps both rich enough and simple enough to guide understanding and action in enabling change.

The nature of this development path

We have found that although some people may set out to work with organizational change as the goal of their development, many emerge somewhere along this third path as a consequence of cumulative experience as trainers, training consultants or learning consultants. Often these are people who start to recognize trends in their work and by focusing on these more directly, they begin to accelerate their development. We look at how this can happen in each case.

Training experience

The evolution here occurs when trainers recognize that people *change* in becoming more competent. Odd as it may seem, many trainers do not see their work in these terms. They regard training as 'giving managers more tools for their kit bag'. The new ideas, techniques and approaches that participants are introduced to on courses stay firmly instrumental. There is a collusive element at work here which allows everyone to avoid the potentially disturbing possibility of personal change, in favour of a non-threatening rationalization, whereby participants leave with some extra bits and pieces at their disposal, but remain fundamentally untouched themselves. With this frame of reference, problems only arise if the tools on offer are not relevant to participants or if they are not clearly understood; in either case the implication is that the trainer's research or presentation is at fault.

The more trainers engage with participants before, during and after courses, the less adequate this approach is likely to seem. Trainers discover how very differently people perceive the same experience; how difficult the application of certain ideas and behaviours will be for some; how resistant one person might be to seeing any value in an approach that another seizes with alacrity. It becomes apparent to trainers that they are dealing with a whole range of non-rational responses to the possibility of personal readjustment. They see the need to understand how people change and to develop refined skills and insights for intervening helpfully in this process. They may turn to psychology for theories based on behavioural, psychoanalytical or humanistic schools of thought, and to the professional field of counselling and therapy for practical application.

As they progress more deeply in working with individual change, their own and others, they may also feel the need to reflect more rigorously on their own role in organizations. They will need to consider how best they can transfer experience gained in a very personal therapeutic context to a business environment without violating ethical and practical considerations. They will decide how implicitly or explicitly they will address personal change issues. They will realize that there are many influences for change shaping each individual, and that people cannot be understood separately from their environment.

In this way training experience in itself may draw someone on to our third development path, in the search for a deeper understanding of individual change in organizational settings.

Consulting experience

An evolution in thinking occurs as consultants stop seeing each project undertaken with a different client manager as a self-contained assignment and start to recognize the links in their work. Finding themselves closer to the realities of the business world, they see the neat formulations which sufficed in the training room give way before the greater complexity of the live situation. They are faced with untangling a number of interrelated variables to distinguish cause and effect. In order to contract effectively for any one assignment they need to recognize a network of organization links, both formal and informal. As they consult with working units rather than train collections of individuals, they discover the need to be concerned as much with the boundary between the unit and the rest of the organization, as with internal group dynamics.

As a result of this experience, consultants become interested in the wider context of their work instead of defining it purely in terms of designing development for a particular group. They draw their working boundaries ever more inclusively as they move from a closed-system perspective to an open-system perspective, introducing them to the fields of organizational behaviour and organization development and various approaches for understanding and planning large-scale organizational change.

Experience with learning-based approaches

It is impossible to develop an appreciation of adult learning and management self-development without dealing with the nature of personal change. In addition, learning consultants focus particularly on creating the *conditions* in which others define and pursue their development goals. As they work with different groups of people in the organization, they help to set up mini-cultures in which learning and self-development can flourish. Such mini-cultures include developmental resources, processes, relationships and policies.

Inevitably, these cultures will be limited and temporary, if consultants do not start working with the wider organizational culture and its impact in blocking or facilitating different kinds of learning. Once they begin to work with managers to make explicit the cultural norms of the organization and to understand how these are maintained and changed, consultants find themselves working with the dynamics of long-term change. They become interested in concepts such as 'the learning organization' and 'organizational culture', and once again become aware that they are on the development path from individual to organizational change.

Comparison with organization development

So far we have looked at the ways people may develop towards organization change consulting from a background in individual management development. It is interesting at this point to see how organization development (OD) has evolved as a profession from its emergence in the 1960s, since it is an approach which has always set out to encompass the whole organization.

OD grew from the application of the behavioural sciences to organizations. It embraced humanistic principles, which counter-balanced the more scientific and mechanistic models of organizational functioning. Just when the idea of continuous change was emerging as the given context in which organizations would have to operate, OD offered the possibility of 'managing' change by implementing long-term, co-ordinated and highly systematic interventions.

In 1969 Richard Beckhard[1] defined OD as 'an effort which is *planned*, *organization-wide*, and *managed* from the *top*, to increase *organization effectiveness* and *health* through interventions based on *behavioural-science* knowledge.' The profession

developed a wealth of intervention strategies, a whole technology of change based primarily on:

-   Working with *groups* as the basic building blocks of an
    organization.
-   Working on *intergroup* relationships between subsystems.
-   Working on *planning* and *goal-setting* processes.
-   Working on *educational* activities for upgrading the know-
    ledge, skill and abilities of *key* personnel.

Fifteen years after Beckhard was writing, Adrian McLean[2] et al.
undertook research into OD as it was *actually* being practised
and concluded that the profession had evolved in a number of
ways. In summary these were:

(a) Far less emphasis on applying well developed theories and
    techniques of change; more emphasis on consultants deve-
    loping their own ideas and approaches to meet each new
    situation.
(b) Less ambitious organization-wide programmes; more
    emphasis on the cumulative effect of smaller projects under-
    taken over time.
(c) Fewer discrete, finite projects; more continuous and seam-
    less activities,
(d) Less evangelism and idealism; more pragmatic acceptance
    of the political realities of organizational life.
(e) Less of the stance of an OD consultant as a neutral, external
    facilitator towards a more active partiality and involvement
    in the change process.
(f) Less emphasis on *planned* change; more emphasis on *plann-
    able* change, i.e. the daily task of addressing issues as they
    arise.
(g) Less emphasis on rational, sequential descriptions of the
    change process; more reliance on intuitive, integrative,
    holistic understanding of the nature of change.

Further evidence of the route along which OD professionals are
developing comes from Robert Tannenbaum and Robert
Hanna.[3] Writing recently about organizational change consulting, they identify the lack of emphasis on the *individual* human

system in traditional OD work, particularly the individual in transition. 'The nature of any system change and the degree to which it is realized, ultimately depend upon the unique responses of the individuals involved in the change.' They highlight the range of studies into the stages of personal transition which accompany significant life changes and crises, all of which follow some pattern of 'holding on, letting go and moving on'. They point out that OD has concentrated primarily on planning and implementing the 'moving on' stage of change, while dealing with 'resistance to change' in relatively superficial ways. As a result important change programs have encountered great difficulty in building up momentum and solidly maintaining it over a period of time.

The authors suggest that OD professionals need to pay more attention to understanding the human processes of 'holding on' and facilitating the ability to 'let go', i.e. dealing with the emotional responses to loss and the attempt to avoid the accompanying pain (e.g. shock, frustration, confusion, anger, helplessness and depression). Helping people work through such reactions requires more than a purely systematic behavioural-science approach.

All this bodes well for those seeking to develop towards organization change consultancy. It would appear that in treading the path from individual change to organizational change, they are likely to meet an OD consultant walking the other way. In fact the path turns out not to be a linear journey, as in Figure 8.1. Rather the area we are exploring is the fertile ground where the two perspectives meet and create new possibilities. See Figure 8.2.

individual _____➤ organization
change   change

Figure 8.1

Developing the capacity to work with organization change

What does it take to work with organization change over and above the knowledge, skills and attitudes described in earlier chapters? Once consultants can develop strong collaborative

Figure 8.2

relationships with clients, can undertake effectively the necessary work in all stages of the consulting cycle, and can create the conditions for self- and mutual-development by enabling managers to learn how to learn, have they acquired all the competences they need? Is the role of change agent in an organization anything more than a flexible combination of the other roles already mentioned? See Figure 8.3.

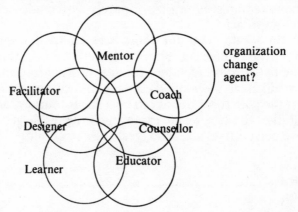

Figure 8.3

In our experience further development *is* needed and at times the extra step can seem large. Those consultants working with organization change testify to the intellectual demand of conceptualizing about organizations, change and the business world, in ways that can inform practical action.

They also find that to remain creative and responsive in

conditions of complex change requires considerable emotional resilience. Finally there is a need for increased autonomy and sense of self based on clarity of purpose and values.

Since this can seem like trying to climb a steep cliff without toe holds, our suggestion for those with limited experience of organization change consulting is to take a fresh look at their skills in constructing and using models for understanding change. Although such a task might appear to be a purely conceptual activity, it is more demanding than it seems and can be invaluable in developing some important capacities for working with organization change. This idea is supported by Gordon Lippitt's list of the attributes of the successful modeller:[4]

1. Personal security – the courage and confidence to step back from a complex situation and trust one's ability to construe it in different ways, rather than become paralysed and confused.
2. Situational sensitivity – above-average capacity to tune in to a situation and perceive a large range of factors at work.
3. Judgement – a willingness to add to, discard or amend a model as the situation develops or new information comes to light.
4. Balance of analysis and synthesis – the ability to break down a situation into parts and relate and combine the parts into meaningful, creative wholes.
5. Tolerance of ambiguity – the ability to work with disorder, paradox and uncertainty while continually searching for meaning. The ability to resist pressure for immediate answers or solutions.

If competence in modelling requires these capacities, then it clearly offers a route for development. The following plan illustrates a sequence which has helped many of the people we have worked with:

(a) Understand the nature of models.
(b) Become conscious of the models, frameworks and principles already underpinning one's current work.
(c) Experiment with using familiar models to generate an organizational perspective.
(d) Learn about a wider range of organizational models.
(e) Create one's own models.

The range of potentially useful models is vast. In the remainder of this chapter we illustrate modelling as a developmental activity rather than attempting any kind of inventory. Our intention is to stimulate the reader's thinking about this approach to developing self or others as organization change consultants.

Understanding the nature of models

We all have cognitive maps which govern the meaning we make of any situation and so enable us to decide on purposeful action. The emphasis here is on the word purposeful. It is possible to leap straight from the experience of a situation into action, but it is the stage of reflection and meaning-making which informs and guides action. For the consultant it is the quality of the meaning-making which underwrites the design of effective change interventions. This is where models come in: 'In simple terms a model is a way of *representing* a complex situation so as to define certain aspects of it and their interrelationships'.[5]

Models are at the heart of the work of the organization change consultant. They enable him or her to:

- *Describe* a complex situation, and highlight where information is needed.
- *Interpret* the situation, through the interrelationships inherent in the model, leading to clearer understanding and diagnosis.
- *Design* ways of intervening in a situation as the model allows assessment of the consequences of action.
- *Communicate* with others about the situation and develop shared perceptions.

The consulting cycle referred to in Chapter 4 is a model of the consulting process which isolates six activities and links them sequentially in a cycle, i.e. a typical *schematic* model, as is an organizational chart which depicts the hierarchical relationships between roles in a company management structure. Models can also be *concrete* (such as the scaled-down replica of a production plant), *abstract* (such as mathematical symbols linked by a formula, e.g. H_2O is an abstract model of water) or *analogous* (such as thinking of an organization as a machine designed to deliver certain products).

It is helpful to recognize that all models are metaphorical, that they suggest a way of seeing that simultaneously makes certain aspects of a situation more visible while blinding the observer to other aspects. For example, as mentioned above, one way of representing an organization is an organization chart (Figure 8.4). The model draws attention to such aspects of the organization as the division of tasks and responsibilities, reporting structures, spans of control, the formal power structure and lines of formal communication.

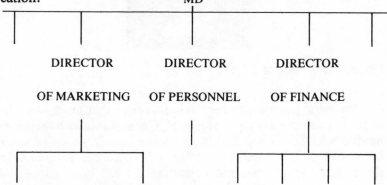

Figure 8.4   Organization chart

Another model of an organization (Figure 8.5) is the simple open systems model. This model stimulates questions about suppliers, raw materials, financial resources, market conditions, products, monitoring systems, quality control, internal systems and procedures.

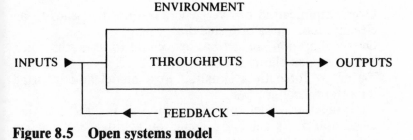

Figure 8.5   Open systems model

The organization chart model is static, emphasizing structure; the systems model is dynamic, emphasizing exchange and process. Both are 'true', both are valuable and both are partial. As with the Gestalt psychologists'[6] experiments with perception we can only construe the world one way at a time. In the well known example shown in Figure 8.6 at any moment we can *either* see a vase *or* see two faces in profile, but not both together.

Figure 8.6   Vase or Faces?

From what has already been said it is clear that models can be as great a liability as they are an asset. Consultants with favourite models will gain a reputation for doing certain kinds of work because they will always construe organizational issues in the same way. Many external consultants have built successful businesses by marketing the approaches that flow from particular models – clients know in advance what they are likely to become involved in when they invite in certain consultants. For the internal consultant it seems to us particularly important not to become attached to a limited range of models that become a biased way of seeing.

There are other possible dangers in modelling:

- Over-simplification or over-generalization that leads to an elegant model but a distorted diagnosis.
- Over-elaboration, an attempt to account for everything in a model, so that clarity is lost.
- Trying to force fit a situation to a model and ignoring important incongruities.
- Allowing the model to become an end in itself, so that discussion of its validity becomes an avoidance of dealing with the actual situation.

- Over-emphasizing the objectivity of models and failing to recognize the assumptions, beliefs and values implicitly incorporated in them.

We hope that what we have said so far gives some idea of the enabling and paradoxically constraining nature of models.

Becoming conscious of models in use

Anyone working in the field of human resource development will already have a whole range of theories and rationales underpinning their work. These may cover leadership, conflict, group development, motivation, learning, communication, teamwork, management, change, selection, assessment and so on. The next stage of the consultant's development is recognizing how these ideas are providing models which inform his or her current practice.

When asked 'What model (a group, an effective team, a successful planning process) were you using in designing this development activity?', it is surprising how many trainers we have worked with will look blank and reply 'I do not know that I was using any model'. The key words are 'I do not know'. If the design is not random, then behind it will be some kind of model, even if the trainer is unconscious of this. Further probing and 'unpacking' of the consultant's approach will invariably elicit the underlying models.

Initially people often need help in this kind of self-questioning. Although at first they may feel under test to 'prove' what they know, with genuine interest and encouragement, most people's self-confidence blossoms as they engage in a process which helps them to realize how much they have already internalized. They become more rigorous and purposeful and more aware of the relation between their own framing of a situation and the work they do.

We talked with one internal consultant about a team-building event she was designing. Initially she declared that the design was based on R. M. Belbin's[7] research into team roles (Belbin suggested that people adopt one or more preferred roles in a team from a possible range of eight, each of which provides a valuable contribution to the team's ability to perform its tasks), but in further discussions with her it became clear that she was drawing on a number of other models without being fully aware of it.

- In considering who should be included in the team-building event, and also the extent to which internal relationships should be emphasized rather than the organizational context, she was drawing on her knowledge of *boundaries*.[8]
- In making decisions on how to manage the risk level she had a model of *group development*[9] in mind.
- In designing the flow of exercises and reviews she was influenced by *Kolb's learning cycle*.[10]

By bringing the underlying models to the surface she could immediately see where her design could be improved. It became clear to her where certain sequences of sessions were inappropriate and where she could meet several objectives simultaneously.

Experimenting with familiar models

We have seen many trainers paralyse themselves when faced with organizational work because they have rushed to an OD textbook in search of a method for organizational analysis, and then tried to apply approaches which they only partially understand. Although the models they have relied on to date will not be sufficient for organization change consulting, they provide a valuable starting point and they are at least imbued with the richness of real experience.

For example, a purely intrapersonal model may be useful for assessing aspects of organizational 'personality' or culture. Interpersonal models can help to diagnose interdepartmental issues. Developmental or life-stage models can illuminate the 'maturity' of an organization and its readiness for change. Models of adult learning can throw light on the idea of learning organizations. Frameworks for understanding the role of the individual counsellor can throw light on the relationship of consultant to total client system.

We now give some examples of the initial thoughts of trainers when asked to describe aspects of their organization using familiar models that they would usually apply to individuals or training groups. In each case some pointers towards diagnosis and action emerged, and it was clear that these pointers increased the trainers' confidence in their ability to begin working at an organizational level.

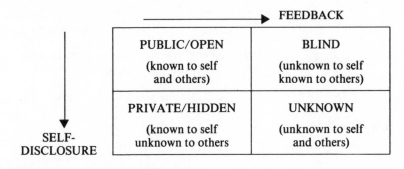

Figure 8.7   Johari Window

Example (1): The Johari Window[11]   The model (Figure 8.7) was originally conceived to describe the self in interaction with others. The model suggests that self-disclosure to others and feedback from others considerably increases the area of effective 'free' activity and also slowly uncovers the unconscious potential of the individual.

This model was used by a training consultant to clarify his perceptions of the climate in a client company prior to reorganization of the field service operation. His task was to design courses to educate and train staff for their new roles and responsibilities. His data came from interviews with key personnel, both those instigating the change strategy and those affected by it.

He adapted the Johari Window as shown in Figure 8.8. He sorted the information and perceptions he had accumulated into the model. In general terms it then looked as it does in Figure 8.9.

As he was encouraged to think in terms of a longer-term intervention strategy rather than a series of training courses, this consultant identified some options for proposals he could discuss with his clients:

ORGANIZATIONAL AWARENESS →

PUBLIC	BLIND
Openly acknowledged. Clear to me and the organization.	Perceived by me, but the organization seems unaware.
HIDDEN	UNKNOWN
Privately acknowledged to me, but not made public.	Unclear to me or the organization.

ORGANIZA-
TIONAL
DISCLOSURE

Figure 8.8

PUBLIC/OPEN	BLIND
Published information and policy statements about the reasons for reorganization, the benefits of the proposed new structures. Existence of large numbers of rumours acknowledged. Some new appointments made.	To aspects of current culture that are inimical to the changes. To commonality of unvoiced concerns. To incompleteness of formal communications about changes. To paralysing effect of sense of powerlessness in parts of the organization.
PRIVATE/HIDDEN	UNKNOWN
Individual anxiety about career prospects. No discussion of the consequences of changes. Lack of certainty amongst decision-making management of final shape of changes. Criticism and suggestion not expressed upwards, only to peers.	Capacity to discover and devise new ways of working which release energy and motivation.

Figure 8.9

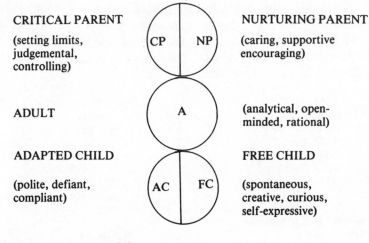

CRITICAL PARENT

(setting limits, judgemental, controlling)

NURTURING PARENT

(caring, supportive encouraging)

ADULT

(analytical, open-minded, rational)

ADAPTED CHILD

(polite, defiant, compliant)

FREE CHILD

(spontaneous, creative, curious, self-expressive)

Figure 8.10   TA model

1. Offer to work with the management team to help them clarify remaining uncertainties about the change strategy and to design a more effective communication process.
2. Suggest third-party facilitation of a consultative meeting between members of the management team and field staff to hear responses to and suggestions for improving the change plans.
3. Design a series of change implementation workshops attended by vertical slices of the organization instead of horizontal slices attending training courses as originally planned; devise a problem-solving approach where groups identify and work on some of the perceived blocks to the successful implementation of the changes.

Example (2): Transactional Analysis (TA)[12]   One of the fundamentals in TA is the analysis of individual functioning in terms of three ego states (parent, adult and child), each of which describes a coherent pattern of thoughts, feelings and behaviours. The model represents an individual as in Figure 8.10.

The model suggests that it is possible to construct ego-grams to represent the relative use of different ego states by an individual and to analyse characteristic ways in which each type of ego state is manifested.

A trainer used this idea to describe her organization, an insurance company. She then considered what new insight this gave her into the reasons why two interventions currently being implemented by the T and D department were meeting with very different degrees of success. See Figure 8.11.

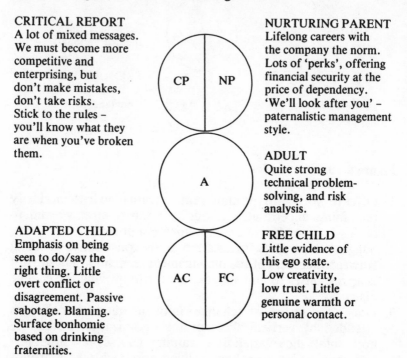

CRITICAL REPORT
A lot of mixed messages. We must become more competitive and enterprising, but don't make mistakes, don't take risks. Stick to the rules – you'll know what they are when you've broken them.

NURTURING PARENT
Lifelong careers with the company the norm. Lots of 'perks', offering financial security at the price of dependency. 'We'll look after you' – paternalistic management style.

ADULT
Quite strong technical problem-solving, and risk analysis.

ADAPTED CHILD
Emphasis on being seen to do/say the right thing. Little overt conflict or disagreement. Passive sabotage. Blaming. Surface bonhomie based on drinking fraternities.

FREE CHILD
Little evidence of this ego state. Low creativity, low trust. Little genuine warmth or personal contact.

Figure 8.11

The two interventions were both attempts to change the management style of the company in the light of new conditions in the financial market place. The company recognized the need to move from a bureaucratic to a more flexible, initiative-taking, customer-orientated culture.

One method was to provide interpersonal skills training courses for the middle management layers in the company, with an emphasis on building more open working relationships. These programmes were foundering in a morass of anger, suspicion and fear. Despite careful pre-course briefing, during which potential participants appeared willing and interested in attending (saying the right thing), those leading the programmes were repeatedly faced with passively hostile groups unwilling to work with the material.

From her analysis the trainer could see clearly that the courses were aimed at activating the free child ego states, the least robust and supported aspect of the company's 'personality'. There had been no attempt to address the negative effects of the parental messages. The programme rationale, which might have been expected to appeal to the adult ego states was based on humanistic, self-awareness concepts, which were basically alien to the culture. In all, the course fed directly into and actually reinforced the adapted child it was attempting to change.

A second initiative, based on analytical problem-solving and innovative teamwork, was much more successful. This built on the adult ego state by engaging managers in joint problem-solving on real business issues, using structured techniques. The difficult critical parent and adapted child areas were bypassed, while the free child was gently opened up by introducing cross-functional working, emphasizing joint problems rather than personalities and encouraging acceptance and curiosity in one another's ideas and potential contributions.

Example (3): Kolb's learning cycle   David Kolb's model of the learning process (Figure 8.12) identifies four essential activities. He also suggests that individuals will have preferred learning styles and particular blocks to learning.

Figure 8.12   Kolb's learning cycle

Ben Bennett and Jim Richardson[13] applied this model to organizations to show how different kinds of culture or structure could block different aspects of the learning cycle. See Figure 8.13.

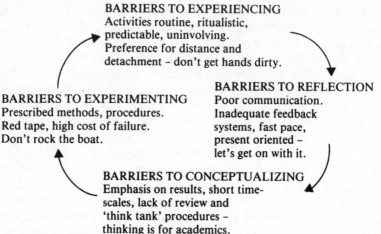

BARRIERS TO EXPERIENCING
Activities routine, ritualistic, predictable, uninvolving.
Preference for distance and detachment – don't get hands dirty.

BARRIERS TO REFLECTION
Poor communication.
Inadequate feedback systems, fast pace, present oriented – let's get on with it.

BARRIERS TO EXPERIMENTING
Prescribed methods, procedures.
Red tape, high cost of failure.
Don't rock the boat.

BARRIERS TO CONCEPTUALIZING
Emphasis on results, short time-scales, lack of review and 'think tank' procedures – thinking is for academics.

Figure 8.13   Barriers to learning

In discussions with organizations on the design of a change strategy, which inevitably means learning new ways of working, this model aids diagnosis of the kind of activities the organization most needs to engage in, because they are the ones most likely to be blocked or avoided at present. The principle is to design interventions that will engage the organization members in the less familiar learning styles as well as those which fit the structure and culture of the company. For example, some organizations can spend too much time reflecting and conceptualizing, through the over-use of committees and by constant reference of decisions up the hierarchy. They may need to be encouraged to experiment with pilot projects.

Learning about a wider range of organizational models

This step involves familiarization with models designed specifically to deal with organizational systems rather than individuals or groups. In fact trainers are often well acquainted with some of these in the sense that they introduce managers to them on courses; the development involves trainers in actually applying them to organizational issues. An example might be Kurt Lewin's force field analysis.[14] See Figure 8.14.

Figure 8.14   Force field analysis

This model represents any situation as a dynamic equilibrium between opposing forces. By analysing the range and strength of forces acting in the status quo, trainers may discover possibilities for action in terms of:

- Introducing new driving forces.
- Reducing or redirecting restraining forces.
- Increasing driving forces (without creating an equal and opposite increase in restraining forces).

Although trainers are often familiar with this model as a problem-solving tool, they may be less aware of its value in mapping organizational dynamics in relation to a change goal.

Many other models for organizational diagnosis are derived from systems theory. They invite analysis in terms of the relationships between organizational inputs, outputs, throughputs, environment and feedback/monitoring systems. One such example is the model developed by Graham Pratt and Bob Lees (Figure 8.15). They use it in collaboration with their clients to arrive at a joint diagnosis. Below are some of the questions they might pose:

1. *Purpose.* What is the basic reason for the existence of the organization? Are people satisfied with this purpose? Is it related to environmental needs?
2. *Organizational strategy.* What is the general direction which the organization will pursue in order to achieve its purpose?

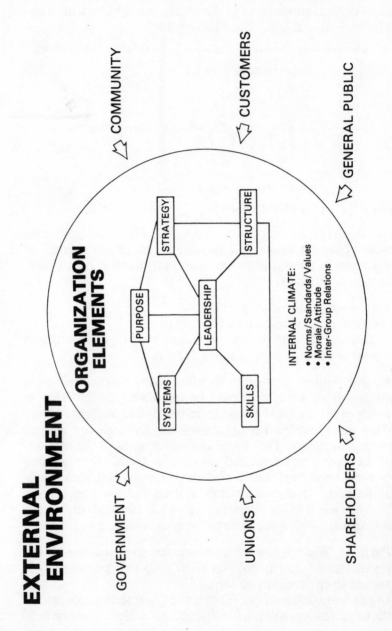

Figure 8.15   Pratt/Lees model

3. *Structure*. What is the relationship of the various functions to each other in the whole organization? Are there too many levels for effective communication? Are people comfortable with today's structure? Should it be changed to support a new strategy and purpose? Are there some new roles that need to be developed?

4. *Systems*. Are regularly interacting and interdependent groups of activities forming a united whole? (Examples are work flow, job design, information flow, decision-making systems, committees/meetings, technology.)

5. *Skills*. What is the ability of individuals or work units to use knowledge and experience effectively in performing tasks or making decisions? Is there the necessary mix of managerial and technical skills to meet the challenge of the future? If the organization is changing, are any new skills needed?

6. *Internal climate*. What are the norms of generalized or collective behaviour in the organization? Are they changing? Do they need to change? What is valued, believed in by the members of the organization? As change takes place are there any values which need to be protected? If so, how? How effective are the relations between the different teams, divisions and departments in the organization?

7. *Leadership*. Do the leaders have a long-term vision for the organization? What types of leadership would support the organization's efforts to adjust to change?

8. *External environment*. Who are the outside parties that significantly affect the way the organization does its business? Does anything need to be done to improve relationships with any of these groups?

Other types of models fall into one or another of Gareth Morgan's [15] classification of organizational metaphors:

- Organizations as machines focusing on efficiency and rationality.
- Organizations as cultures focusing on history, rituals, beliefs and norms.
- Organizations as political systems focusing on power, competition and vested interests.

- Organizations as psyches focusing on patterns of unconscious processes.
- Organizations as organisms focusing on interdependence, growth and development.
- Organizations as brains focusing on creativity, information-processing and problem-solving.
- Organizations as flux and transformation focusing on change processes.

Sometimes trainers feel overwhelmed at the complexity of some of these models, mistakenly believing that, in order to use them, they need to know about all aspects of a company. In fact the value of models to organization change consultants is in helping them formulate pertinent questions about the organization's functioning. The answers lie with their clients, and the model then provides a way of sorting the information as an aid to joint diagnosis and to intervention design.

Creating one's own models

Once consultants stop being overawed by models, they become increasingly able to 'play' with them as liberating and effective tools for gaining fresh insights into organizational issues. Some models may be creative and metaphorical, e.g. representing interdepartmental relationships as an extended family. These 'models' emerge simply from a willingness to be uninhibited and to say 'This state of affairs is just like . . .'. Very often in fitting aspects of the actual situation to the metaphor, the trainer finds that the model breaks down, but its usefulness lies in the discussion it generates and the possible interrelationships of cause and effect it suggests.

Other models are created by the more painstaking process of arranging and rearranging information about a situation, grouping certain aspects, ordering, classifying and symbolizing until a coherent framework begins to emerge. The analysis becomes a useful model once the representation of the situation becomes recognizable to others in the organization and invites discussion and hypothesis.

Clarity of purpose

At the beginning of this chapter we mentioned increased breadth and depth as necessary features of the development path from individual to organizational change. We have suggested that consultants need to develop ways of thinking about organizations, through the use of diagnostic models. Taking the view that all action by consultants in a client system is an intervention means that clarity of purpose is vital, if consultants are not to become hopelessly entangled in the complexities of the system they are working with. Organization models provide one way of keeping sight of the wood when deep among the trees.

Clarity of purpose is also based on awareness of one's own aims and beliefs, which comes from knowing the answers to such questions as:

- 'What sort of organizations do I want to help create?'
- 'What sort of work do I really want to do?'
- 'What sort of relationships do I want to build with my clients?'
- 'What values underpin my work?'
- 'How will I handle organizational politics?'
- 'Are there certain assignments I will refuse?'
- 'How will I resolve questions of confidentiality?'

Consultants with some clarity about their own purpose are likely to be better equipped to help their clients define the longer-term future of the companies they manage, an essential aspect of the work of organization change consultants.

Notes

1. Beckhard R. *ORGANIZATION DEVELOPMENT: STRATEGIES AND MODELS*, Addison-Wesley 1969.
2. McLean A. J., Sims D. B. P., Maugham I. L., Tuffield. *ORGANIZATION DEVELOPMENT IN TRANSITION – EVIDENCE OF AN EVOLVING PROFESSION* Wiley 1982.
3. Tannenbaum R. (ed.). *HUMAN SYSTEMS DEVELOPMENT*, Jossey Bass 1985.
4. Lippitt G. L., *VISUALIZING CHANGE: MODEL BUILDING AND THE CHANGE PROCESS*, University Associates 1973.

5. Lippitt, ibid.
6. Kohler W. *GESTALT PSYCHOLOGY*, New American Library 1975.
7. Belbin R. M. *MANAGEMENT TEAMS: WHY THEY SUCCEED OR FAIL*, Heinemann 1981.
8. Phillips K., 'Boundaries and Boundary Management in Interpersonal Skills Training', *JOURNAL OF EUROPEAN AND INDUSTRIAL TRAINING*, Vol. 7, No. 3, 1983.
9. Porter L. and Mohr (eds). *READING BOOK FOR HUMAN RELATIONS TRAINING*, N. T. L. Institute 1982.
10. Kolb D. et al., op. cit.
11. Porter and Mohr, op. cit.
12. Barker D. *TA AND TRAINING*, Gower 1980.
13. Bennett B. and Richardson J., 'Applying Learning Techniques to on-the-job Development', *JOURNAL OF EUROPEAN AND INDUSTRIAL TRAINING*', Vol. 8, No. 1, 1984.
14. Lewin K. *FIELD THEORY IN SOCIAL SCIENCE*, Harper and Row 1951.
15. Morgan G. *IMAGES OF ORGANIZATION*, Sage 1986.

9 The Organization Change Consultant

This chapter describes in more detail the consulting project, extending over one year, outlined briefly in Chapter 2. It is chosen to illustrate how an initial request for training courses had the potential for an organization change intervention. Although we undertook the project as external consultants, it is likely to be similar in its starting point to the situation facing many trainers moving into internal consulting roles. Often their potential clients will still expect them to provide training courses for individuals, but if their own perspective is that of organizational change, they will be able to widen the scope of their work.

An organization change assignment

Initial contact

We received a telephone call from Adrian Croft, the Head of Training of Bolton-Smith Ltd. He had heard that we ran training courses for trainers becoming consultants; he wanted us to run a similar programme, suitably modified, for IT specialists. We said that the modifications could well be extensive, since the range of skills that trainers would bring to such a programme were likely to be very different from those of computer specialists. That said, we agreed to meet in order to discuss possibilities.

In preparing for the meeting we decided to resist pressure simply to run an in-house version of the open course. We wanted to learn a lot more about the context in which the need for this training had been identified.

When we got to the meeting there were two others present apart from Adrian Croft. These were Geoff Keen, the Personnel Manager, and John Williams, Director of the Information Technology Division.

Essentially the need for consultancy skills training arose out of Bolton-Smith's long established tradition of working as expert technical consultants. They were now discovering the need to work more collaboratively with their clients, and appreciated that such collaboration was one of the most effective ways of securing follow-up work. At present they had too many one-off assignments and their status in the market place was generally 'second division'; they were having difficulty securing assignments in the management consultancy field which they saw as an expanding market.

The IT Division had been identified as the prime target for training, which would then be extended to other divisions, including financial and economic planning and market studies.

In probing for the broader context within which the training was wanted, we learned that the whole strategy for the company was under review. There was, in particular, a debate about whether to:

- Decentralize and set up regional centres.
- Break down the existing divisions and regroup them according to market sectors.
- Set up a separate management consultancy group.

Although the legitimacy of our questions about these broader issues was recognized, our clients still saw us very much as training consultants. We spent some time discussing our role with them, pointing out in particular that the manner in which we worked needed to mirror the aims of the assignment. It was a glaring contradiction for us to operate as prescriptive experts when this was exactly the style of consultancy they wanted to move away from. We explained that in experimenting together with a more collaborative approach we and they would learn a great deal more about the organization's potential difficulties in changing their own consultancy style.

Looking back on the meeting, we realized this was the most critical part of it. Our clients accepted the validity of what we were saying at a cognitive level, but felt anxious about engaging with us in a mode they were unsure how to manage. The greater ambiguity inherent in the consultancy style that they wanted to develop and which they were experiencing with us gave them cause for thought.

The meeting closed with a discussion about fees and our agreement to write a formal proposal. We were told that Geoff Keen would be our client contact for the day-to-day management of the project and he would liaise closely with John Williams; Adrian Croft would be responsible for ultimately guiding the extension of the assignment to the other divisions.

Initial proposal

CONSULTANT DEVELOPMENT IN THE IT DIVISION OF BOLTON-SMITH LTD

PRESENTING SITUATION – the need for change
Bolton-Smith offers services which cover both traditional consultancy and newer areas of activity such as information technology.

Historically, the 'prescriptive' mode of consultation has been used and indeed expected by your clients. You have identified the need for a more flexible collaborative consultancy style to meet the emerging demands of the market place, especially in providing an integrated management consultancy service.

THE FOCUS FOR CHANGE – target population.
At present the need for change is perceived most clearly in the Information Technology Division. John Williams, the divisional director, sees this as an urgent operational requirement in the face of the following situation:

(a) The division is expanding rapidly with an expected intake of 120 people over the next 3 years.

(b) About one-third of this intake is likely to come from the soft-
ware houses or new graduates. These recruits are likely to be highly competent within their technical specialism but will have more limited knowledge, skills and experience of consulting.

(c) Because of the historical situation indicated above, both new recruits with some consulting experience and existing Bolton-Smith staff are likely to be more familiar with a 'prescriptive' consulting style than any other.

Discussions between John Williams, Geoff Keen (Personnel Manager) and Adrian Croft (Director of Training and Recruitment) have resulted in a decision to resource a comprehensive training and development strategy to enhance the consulting skills of the IT Division.

DESIRED OUTCOMES

We believe that some further work is needed to specify these more precisely, but from our discussions so far we identified the following changes as being characteristic of the outcomes you are looking for:

1. *A change in attitude*: the staff in the IT division to see themselves as *consultants* rather than IT specialists. This implies that they understand the nature of the consulting process and recognize that their competence in managing this process is as vital to their effectiveness as their technical knowledge and expertise.

2. *An increase in the level of consulting skill*: consultants to be able to intervene effectively at each stage of the consulting process and to be able to identify and adopt the consultancy style most suitable for different clients and different situations.

3. *A shorter induction period*: new consultants to become fully effective more quickly.

4. *Improved consulting teamwork*: consultants brought together for a particular project to establish effective working teams on the basis of a shared understanding of the aims and methods of consulting in Bolton-Smith.

5. *A reduction in the level of disaffection currently identified among some IT consultants*: consultants to feel well trained,

prepared and supported by Bolton-Smith for the consulting projects they are asked to undertake.

6. *Greater retention of 'able' staff*: consultants to believe that Bolton-Smith offers opportunities for professional development that are not matched by rival firms. This implies that training in consulting skills is part of a wider career development strategy.

We enclose the outlines of two options for addressing these needs. The first represents what we see as the minimum commitment to mount a pilot training event, followed by a series of training courses. The second option sees consulting skills training as part of a wider change intervention. Clearly, there are a number of other possibilities which would combine elements from both options.

OPTION 1
Training to meet the immediate need

1. Identification of training needs by:
   (a) Further discussions with Geoff Keen and John Williams.
   (b) Interviews with some IT consultants, including both those with considerable experience and those relatively new to the division.

At this stage we would be able to judge whether the training needs could all be met within a single mixed-ability training event. Alternatively the needs might be sufficiently diverse to require two distinct modules: the first, an introduction to consultancy skills for new entrants, the second an advanced programme for more experienced consultants.

2. Establishing specific training objectives.
3. Designing, running and evaluating a pilot training event. The course design and content will be based on aspects of the consultancy cycle as described below:

Stages in consultancy	Related issues
1. Gaining entry.	How to establish credibility (dealing with early impressions, past reputations and stereotyped assumptions).

2. Building a working relationship and contracting.	How to clarify mutual expectations and responsibilities.
3. Clarifying purpose and desired outcomes.	How to test and develop commitment.
4. Data collection and diagnosis.	How to deal with issues of trust, conflict, anxiety, status etc.
5. Designing strategies and plans for achieving desired outcomes.	How to engage in joint problem-solving. How to identify and harness organizational resources.
6. Monitoring implementation and identifying possible follow-up.	How to avoid mutual dependency.
7. Disengagement.	How to obtain closure.

4. Estimate of the time required
   (a) Identifying training needs   – 3 consultant days
   (b) Establishing objectives
       designing course and
       materials   – 5 consultant days
   (c) Leading programme   – 4 consultant days
   (d) Evaluation and follow-up   – 2 consultant days

5. Implications
   Benefits
   (a) This option could be put into effect quite quickly to meet the urgent current need.
   (b) Data which can be used for further honing of a full training and development strategy will be generated.
   (c) A modular approach (foundation training + follow-up) would provide professional development for IT consultants.
   Concerns
   (a) Course learning may not be fully transferred to consultants' work if there is no general awareness of, and commitment to, the need for a change in consultancy style within the division allied to new business goals.
   (b) The training may be seen as divorced from and unsup-

ported by management practices regarding recruitment, appraisal, career development, administrative systems, marketing strategy and so on.

The second option describes a broader approach to the assignment which takes account of these concerns.

OPTION 2
Changing the consultancy style in the IT division

1. Overview. See Figure 9.1.

2. Estimate of the time required. It is difficult at this stage to estimate the total time needed for the project. We would need to clarify the boundaries of each segment, the nature of our involvement and agree consultant time for each one. For example, the first stage might involve us facilitating a 1- or 2-day meeting of the management team to crystallise the kind of management consultancy service Bolton-Smith wants to be able to offer. With preliminary work this would mean 3 or 4 consultant days.

3. Implications. From our discussions with you, we know that you are already thinking about the change process along these lines. Our reason for seeing this as a separate option is that here the consulting skills training forms part of the overall development strategy *from the outset*, whereas in Option 1, it may well form a first step towards it. The two options have different implications for the nature of our working relationship and mutual expectations.

4. Fees. For either option our fees would be £___, per consultant day + expenses + VAT.

Commentary on the proposals

1. They emphasize the organizational context within which the training is intended to take place.
2. They concentrate on outcomes rather than means, thereby allowing scope for extensive collaboration with the client in the design and management of the project.

Figure 9.1

3. We offered both a training consultancy and an organizational change consultancy option, giving the client a sense of the possible scope of the project while also offering some limited first steps (a pilot training programme or a management strategy meeting) where our relationship could be tested before further commitment was made.

There was a month's delay before we received a formal response to our proposals. A follow-up call with Geoff Keen revealed that further discussions with more senior management were taking place. Eventually we were invited to take part in an exploration of 'options somewhere between 1 and 2 as outlined in your proposals'. This involved:

(a) Meeting the Managing Director to discuss how our proposals fitted into plans for creating a new management consulting group.
(b) Extending the project to cover all divisions that would form part of this new group.
(c) Undertaking data collection interviews with a selection of consultants from all the divisions, some new to Bolton-Smith, others experienced consultants. Geoff Keen organized the interview schedule and briefed participants about the background.
(d) Scheduling a feedback meeting with the MD and divisional directors at which further plans would be discussed.

Data collection and diagnosis

In our interviews with the consultants we were seeking information about:
1. Consultancy as it was actually practised in Bolton-Smith.
2. In what way, if at all, management consultancy was seen as different from technical consulting.
3. How prepared and able consultants felt to undertake management consultancy.
4. The extent to which consultants felt supported in their work with clients by the organizational structure and practices of Bolton-Smith.

5. How much awareness there was of the changes being discussed at senior levels.
6. The consultants' own perceptions of the need for change in
Bolton-Smith.

Bearing in mind that we were acting as consultants to consultants, we also asked each person, towards the end of the
interview, for comments on our approach and how it was similar
or different from the way in which they might have handled the
interviews themselves. What was most interesting about this was
that no one we spoke to had drawn a parallel between our work
with Bolton-Smith as an organization and their own work with
clients. It was clear that they saw themselves as problem-solvers
not change agents.

The interview data provided some insight into the internal
climate:

- Little liaison between divisions, manifested by unwillingness
  to share information, or pass on work and by ignorance and
  discounting of each other's activities.
- High value placed on individual autonomy and responsibility. Attempts at teamwork unsatisfactory because of individual competitiveness. Issues arising in teams inadequately
  addressed. Lack of team membership and leadership skills
  perceived.
- Senior managers out and about a lot with clients, devoting
  little time to internal management.
- Individuals identify with high professional standards in their
  field, but have little sense of what it means to be a Bolton-
  Smith consultant. Lack of shared purpose and values or
  identification with company.
- No common understanding of the nature of management
  consultancy.
- No targeting for type and quality of assignments. Getting in
  business of any kind is the priority.

With the data generated so far we put together a summary of the
situation as we saw it, using the Pratt–Lees model described in
the previous chapter (pp. 119–21). See Figure 9.2.

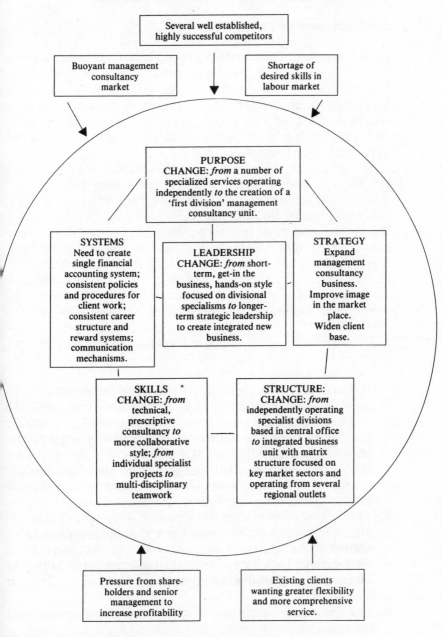

Figure 9.2   Application of Pratt/Lees Model

Feedback meeting with clients

At this meeting with the MD and divisional directors we presented the data and invited responses and discussion. The reaction to this was very positive, even though we were simply presenting to the directors what had been said to us. It was clear that in so doing we were making explicit things which had never been fully articulated or openly discussed, and so had remained apparently unmanageable.

The directors, like their own consultants, were far more comfortable dealing with technical matters related to their specialisms than with issues related to the culture and climate of the company. Indeed they did not really have a language for doing this. It was also clear that there was a big communication gap between the senior management group and the consulting staff. The former did little to elicit information or response from staff, although they were very interested in the data we presented. Their notion of management communication was one way, top-down, and limited to the occasional circulation of written memoranda.

From the discussion we logged agreement on the following points:

1. It would be impossible to divorce the development of consulting skills from the wider issues of change in the company. The move to management consultancy represented a drastic revision of the aims and nature of consulting work as currently practised. Although skill development was necessary for increasing consultant confidence in the non-technical aspects of their work, it would not suffice in creating the new kind of consultancy the directors wanted.
2. The lack of emphasis on collaborative work with clients was mirrored by lack of collaboration within the company. Both needed to be addressed simultaneously so that there was a consistency of working practice internally and externally. The proposed multi-disciplinary team approach would founder without this.
3. Full and visible direction and support would be needed from the management team in leading the change.
4. Involvement of consultant staff in the planning process

would gain commitment to and identification with the new business group.

Design work

The next stage of the contract was to design a development strategy in collaboration with Geoff Keen. Instead of running a training course in consultancy skills, the plan was to bring together a group of consultants who had the potential to create and carry forward a change programme. Geoff Keen had the task of selecting key people from all the divisions who were sources of influence because of their experience, position, ability or personality. We undertook to prepare an outline design proposal for a residential workshop.

At our next meeting with Geoff Keen, pursuing the collaborative approach, we arrived with our design proposals on large pieces of flip-chart paper with options and areas of uncertainty clearly visible. Although a little surprised at first, since his own model of expert consultancy inclined him to expect us to arrive with a polished formal proposal, he was soon involved with us, marker in hand, in amending and building on our design ideas.

By the end of the meeting he was enthusiastic and had a sense of ownership of the design. He was keen to present it to the directors as a joint proposal. He had undertaken to research and prepare certain aspects of the workshop and was willing to take a leading role during it.

We discussed with him the assignment's progress and he began to talk about what he had noticed about our approach, comparing it with the more prescriptive style common in Bolton-Smith. He agreed that he would be willing to discuss these perceptions openly on the workshop.

The workshop design addressed four areas, as shown in Figure 9.3. The key features of the design were:

1. The workshop was to be opened by the managing director giving the background to the project, outlining the plans for the management consultancy group, identifying areas of uncertainty and inviting the group to influence the future direction of the business. This would be done through the

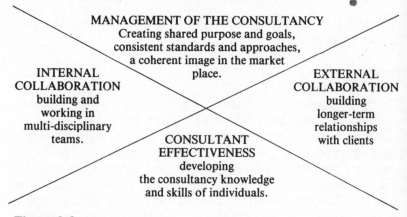

MANAGEMENT OF THE CONSULTANCY
Creating shared purpose and goals,
consistent standards and approaches,
a coherent image in the market
place.

INTERNAL
COLLABORATION
building and
working in
multi-disciplinary
teams.

EXTERNAL
COLLABORATION
building
longer-term
relationships
with clients

CONSULTANT
EFFECTIVENESS
developing
the consultancy knowledge
and skills of individuals.

Figure 9.3

presentation of ideas and proposals at a meeting with the senior management team on the last day.
2. Various models of consultancy and consulting purposes would be introduced to the group; with these in mind, representatives from each of the divisions would discuss their current work and make presentations. Plenary sessions would examine the differences and the common ground between divisions.
3. Mixed divisional groups would be formed to meet regularly during the week. Their task would be to:
   - Learn about inter-disciplinary teamwork.
   - Support their members in a stock-take of skills and the identification of areas for development.
   - Identify the desired characteristics of management consultancy in Bolton-Smith.
   - Work with self-generated and specially prepared case studies so that a common approach could be created for dealing with some of the more typical consulting assignments.
4. As the week progressed the most important issues would be identified and on the penultimate day these would be sifted for relevance in the following day's presentation to senior management. Close attention would be paid to how these ideas, together with recommendations, should be presented; essentially the participants would be acting as internal consultants to the senior management team.

Outcomes from the assignment

In general terms the most significant result of the project was the improvement in communication, both between the senior managers and the rest of the staff and also between the divisions. The directors came to the last morning of the workshop somewhat apprehensive about the possibility of being blamed for the difficulties the consultants were experiencing in their work. The participants themselves feared that their suggestions would simply be swept aside. Since none of these fears were realized, trust grew and some foundations for change within the organization were laid.

Specifically the outcomes were:

- The initiation of cross-divisional meetings to talk about projects and identify areas for collaboration.
- The establishment of two project teams: one to write a draft document articulating the purpose, values and approaches which would characterize consultancy in Bolton-Smith; the other to make proposals for standardized procedures and documentation, when working with clients.
- A presentation by a subset of the consultant group to the management team of the whole organization.
- A follow-up day with the participants to consider the progress so far and to identify further development needs. Three members of the group described in some detail a major success in working collaboratively with a new client.
- A decision to mount another workshop, two of whose features would be:
  - Considering how to direct the business into market sector groups.
  - Some representatives from the previous group would work with us for part of the workshop to pass on the progress made so far and to describe their own experiences in applying their learning.

Postscript

Six months after the events we have described the parent organization took the decision that the management consultancy operations were not viable within the aims of the company and the entire initiative came to a halt – thus underlining some of the points made in the previous chapter about organization change consultancy, in particular that the consultants' working boundaries need to be drawn as inclusively as possible. In this case we gave scant attention to the boundary between the management consultancy and the rest of the firm. Instead, we concentrated on the apparently successful changes taking place, ignoring the larger context and the forces within it which were not supportive of those changes.

We also allowed ourselves to be lulled into dropping our original proposal for initial work with the management consultancy's directors to clarify and strengthen their strategy. As we have illustrated here, working in the interstices of an organization to create change from the bottom up can be very effective; but in the end, if it is not accompanied by equivalent work from the top down, then new initiatives will always be vulnerable.

Epilogue: From Doing to Engaging

We pondered for some time on what we wanted to write by way of a conclusion for this book, and we have decided to concentrate on the most significant change we are aware of in our own development as consultants, i.e. we now see our effectiveness not purely in terms of what we know or what we do, rather more in terms of *how* we work with clients. This is something we have talked about with many others interested in the question of what makes consultants effective in working with individual organizational change. It is not easy to describe this shift in simple and concrete terms. Some may find in our ideas an echo and confirmation of their own experience; others may find them rather esoteric; but we hope at least to stimulate curiosity.

The nature of paradigm shifts

The change from a 'doing' to an 'engaging' orientation as a consultant is a paradigm shift. In this sense it is unlike the other forms of change that occur in the process of development as new challenges are encountered. Most of the time change is effected within an existing paradigm by such processes as:

1. Change by exception: this idea or situation does not fit an

141

exisiting way of understanding things but after momentary confusion is incorporated as the exception which proves the rule.

2. Pendulum change: change by conversion. The previous ideas, methods and so on are rejected as wrong and new ones embraced as the 'truth'.
3. Incremental change: change achieved step by step; a bit more or less of the same.
4. Transition: a gradual change from one set of conditions to another by a process of letting go of some aspects of the old and integrating the new.

Each of these types of change offers a way of handling unsettling novelty. Some are more developmental than others: in pendulum change one set of introjects may replace another, whereas in the process of transition there is assimilation.

The less common experience of paradigm shift often occurs when new ideas or situations create conflicts within the existing paradigm that threaten its continuing validity. Someone experiencing these conditions can relieve the distress in two ways:

–   *Either*: protect the existing paradigm by avoiding, denying or distorting the disturbing stimulus.
–   *Or*: restructure one's understanding at a higher level of organization which is capable of resolving the conflict.

As an example, let us look at one way in which these conditions could arise in practice.

Paradigm A: 'Having/doing' as a basis for competence

Original situation   'I have worked as an internal consultant in this small organization for three and a half years. I have built up a lot of knowledge about how it operates and have used my skills to help many individuals and groups become more effective. I am confident of my contribution in terms of the cumulative effect of my activities and the various change programmes I have seeded. I would like to move to another organization in order to undertake similar work in more challenging circumstances.'

New situation   After moving to the new post, the consultant experiences a drop in confidence. This new organization is large, diverse and complex. She knows so little about it. Her early activities seem like drops in the ocean. There are times when the whole notion of herself as an individual enabling the change and development of an organization seems ludicrous. She wards off the anxiety by remembering how confident she felt in her last job. She tells herself it is just a matter of time, that a drop in confidence and competence in job transition is a well known phenomenon. She redoubles her efforts to find out about the organization, make new contacts and build up a history of successful activity.

Paradigm shift   After a couple of months, while reviewing her progress she feels a moment of despair. It is going to take too long to reach the same level of competence she had before. She needs to be competent *now* not at some future date, but she cannot do any more than she is doing to accelerate her development. Her way of understanding her work is failing her. Old certainties are becoming vague and slipping out of her grasp. Her mind either races or goes blank. In the words of Marilyn Ferguson: 'Confusion, fear, tension, pain and paradox are transformations trying to happen'.[1] She needs another way of understanding her work.

Paradigm B: 'Engaging' as a basis for competence

'I am an internal consultant in this organization. I bring to my work more than knowledge, skills and experience; I bring myself. Just as I change in my contacts with my environment, my environment changes in contact with me. The possibility of development exists in that contact, in the engagement. In paying close attention to the relationship between myself as I am, my clients as they are, in the situation as it is, I am, paradoxically, focusing on the point of maximum possibility – of what can be.

'When I look at my work in this way, valid data, diagnosis, design and intervention exist in each unfolding moment of my relationship with my clients as well as over a period of time. My effectiveness is actual as well as potential. I do not need to wait until I have found out more and done more things in order to have an impact or to have influence. This supersedes but does not negate my previous understanding of how to be effective.'

The consultant as organizational therapist

The ideas in this second paradigm will be familiar to many therapists. Firstly, most therapies share the concept of the primacy of the therapeutic relationship as the crucible in which learning and change takes place.

Secondly, family therapists whose contract is with a system of individuals will be aware of designing interventions with one part of the system that are simultaneously interventions in the whole system. They do not believe they need always to be working directly with all parts of the system to achieve change.

Thirdly, therapists have their own version of the holographic principle, that data about the functioning of the whole are enfolded in each of its parts. They also work with the idea of 'parallel process' which suggests that the interaction between therapist and client reveals data about the client's interaction with others. Both ideas enable a therapist to formulate diagnoses and design interventions, without waiting to investigate every aspect of the total system of which their client is a part.

Finally, several therapies, share ideas about the unblocking and enabling function of highly tuned attention to the present moment.

All these ideas give a consultant the possibility of immediate effectiveness *as well as* increased effectiveness over time. The doing paradigm, which is more linear, encompasses only the second possibility. We make the suggestion that the consultant working in the second paradigm can be thought of as an organizational therapist, mainly to make it clear that this is not a soft option. It is not a question of *just* being there and nothing else matters. It means being there in a way that makes everything matter.

Developing beyond roles

The model we introduced early in this book emphasized distinctions between roles and functions and development paths. It provided a structure for our ideas and has helped trainers we have worked with plan their development in terms of what they needed to know, experiences they needed to have, skills they needed to practise and how they needed to do things differently.

Looking back from the epilogue, we see the distinctions dissolve, and it is clear that development along any one path, taken far enough, becomes development along all three. In the early stages, the distinctions *are* important. There is an emphasis on definitions, tools and techniques, a search for role models, a wish for checklists and guidelines, concern about what is and is not appropriate consultant behaviour. There will be interest in discussion about 'Which stage of the consultancy cycle am I in now?'; feedback to a colleague undertaking skill practice might include the comment, 'It looked to me more as if Brian was the consultant at that point and you were the client'. We have worked with someone who said during a dialogue with a client group 'I'm not saying this as a consultant now, I'm just interested to know whether . . .'. Labels are important to people at this stage, e.g. this is *teaching* which is different from *advising*, which is different from *coaching*, which is different from *counselling*, which is different from *facilitating*.

These processes of differentiation are followed by periods of integration in which the distinctions no longer make sense. There is development beyond roles, a point at which someone may find it difficult to articulate clearly what they now understand, because the frameworks and models which originally helped now hinder. The next cycle of development is triggered by beginning to make a completely different set of distinctions which take account of the integration achieved. This is also how we see the distinction between doing and engaging that we have introduced in this epilogue.

Note

1. Ferguson, M. *THE AQUARIAN CONSPIRACY*, Paladin 1982.

Appendix I   Getting Started: A Self-Development Plan for Trainers

The model below indicates four interlinked areas for learning. They are not mutually exclusive; development in one will inevitably affect the other three.

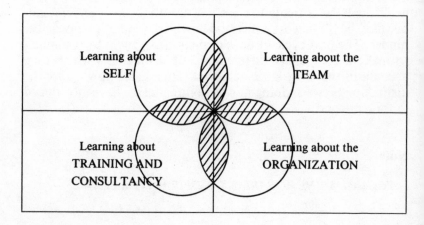

Self

- The capacity to handle uncertainty and ambiguity with confidence and competence requires a willingness to learn about self, i.e. personal style, values, beliefs and preferences.

Training and Consultancy

- A need to learn about, design and run more flexible and experientially based events/sessions/workshops.
- The ability to move out of the training room.
- Learning how to encourage self-development.
- Learning how to manage relationships with a client.

Team

- The team is an important source of stability, support and strategy.
- It can provide a living model of how to work in a collaborative way.
- It is important to learn about individual and collective strengths and weaknesses.

Organization

- Taking a wider perspective; learning to see the organization as an entity.
- Seeing the organization in the context of a changing environment; discovering the trends which affect it.

Methods

The plan contains a variety of different learning methods. In this way you can familiarize yourself with your own preferred way of learning and its assets and liabilities. Some examples of the methods are: guided reading, projects, direct feedback from colleagues, short self-study programmes, course attendance, mentoring, coaching, conducting interviews/surveys; indeed any everyday occurence can be seen as an opportunity for learning.

Detailed Outline

Under each of the four areas there are suggested activities. The first step in developing an individual plan may be the generation of ideas in each of the areas.

Self

Planning time for self-development

- Keep a time log. Decide how much time you will allocate for your own development; begin to set some priorities.
- Complete a computer-based package on time-management.
- Read some books on time-management.[1]

Gaining greater self-awareness

- Tape a training session; use it to carry out a self-assessment which you can then discuss with a colleague.
- Complete a self-awareness questionnaire, e.g. transactional analysis,[2] Myers-Briggs.[3]
- Complete a learning styles inventory.[4]
- Stretch yourself by taking risks during training sessions, e.g. being more confronting or supportive; less directive.
- Attend some personal development programmes.
- Keep a journal of your thoughts and feelings; review it over time and identify any themes.
- Find a co-counselling [5] partner and arrange regular sessions. Use this as an opportunity to explore your feelings and to identify common themes in your work and life.
- Consider engaging in some professional counselling or therapy in order to increase your understanding of yourself.

Assessing your support networks

- Consider the type of support you currently get and from whom – emotional closeness, intellectual stimulation, professional challenge, fun. Assess whether it is adequate for your current needs; where and how you might change and extend it.

Training and consultancy

Knowledge of the variety of self-development techniques

- Get together with some colleagues to brainstorm some ideas.
- Do some reading on self-development[6] and action learning.[7]

- Join or form a self-development group or action learning set.

Knowledge of consultancy

- Assess yourself against a consulting skills checklist (see appendix II).
- Read some books on consultancy.[8]
- Find out who does consultancy in your section/organization; go and interview them to find out what they do and the skills they use.
- Arrange to go out with a consultant as an observer on a client visit.
- Conduct some interviews to practise your data collection skills.

Development of design to incorporate self-development techniques

- Take a session on an existing course and redesign it so that the participants are more responsible for deciding the learning content, while the trainer manages the overall structure.
- Practice having a day of self-directed workshops on standard courses.
- Design pre- and post-courses briefing materials.
- Help a colleague formulate a self-development plan.
- Carry out a post-course counselling session with a manager; follow it with some self-supervision.

Discover how training and consultancy are carried out in other organizations

- Think of some organizations which are similar to yours and others which are very different; arrange to visit some of them.
- Arrange a short period of secondment or an exchange.
- Co-train or co-consult with people from other organizations.
- Network; join your local branches of associations and professional bodies, e.g. AMED,[9] IPM,[10] The Business Network;[11] attend conferences.

Team

Knowledge of your team role

- Complete an inventory on team roles; [12] discuss with your team how your roles relate to each other and the implications for team effectiveness.
- Undertake an assignment which requires your team to work together; use the model of task, procedure and process to review your effectiveness.
- Videotape some of your meetings.
- Invite a consultant to help you review the way you work.

Working with other members of the team

- Create opportunities to work on each others' courses; run some sessions jointly.
- Take time to get to know each other's differences and similarities; arrange a half day where each member of the team writes down on flip chart their skills and experience, what they can offer and what they want from their colleagues. Post these round the room and negotiate wants and offers.

Using the team as a resource base

- Draw up a chart of the organizational networks, both formal and informal, with which each member of the team is in touch.
- Develop a system whereby members of the team can gather and share information about the organizational changes which are taking place.

Organization

Knowledge of organizational models

- Reading.[13]
- Carry out an organizational diagnosis (see Chapter 8).

Learning about the organization's environment

- Interview some senior managers.
- Read the newspapers over a fortnight and draw up a mind map which incorporates the main news items which affect your organization.
- Read in-house journals, abstracts and annual reports.
- Interview members of the public for their views on your organization or the business sector it represents.
- Arrange a visit to one of the client companies of your organization.
- Find out if anybody in your organization is carrying out an organization culture survey.

Being a resource link to the organization

- Review the information which your department receives regularly.
- Discuss with your colleagues ways in which the dissemination of the information could be used to promote training and consultancy.
- Visit other departments and sites within the organization; become 'visible'.
- Explore the possibilities of collaboration with other training and consultancy establishments.
- Identify and build informal influential contacts; discover from them how training and consultancy might be of added value to the organization.

Notes

1. Garratt S. *MANAGING YOUR TIME*, Fontana 1984.
2. Available from Mike Reddy, 90 Church Rd, Woburn Sands, Bucks MK17 8TR.
3. Keirsey D and Bates M. *PLEASE UNDERSTAND ME – CHARACTER AND TEMPERAMENT TYPES*, Prometheus Nemesis Book Co. 1984.
4. Available from Peter Honey and Alan Mumford M.C.B. University Press Ltd, Human Resource Studies, 62, Toller Lane, Bradford BD8 9BY
5. Heron J. *CO-COUNSELLING TEACHERS MANUAL*, Human Potential Research Project, University of Surrey, 1978.

6. Pedler, M, Bourgoyne, J. and Boydell T., *A MANAGERS GUIDE TO SELF DEVELOPMENT*, McGraw-Hill 1978.
7. Pedler M. (ed.) *ACTION LEARNING IN PRACTICE* Gower 1983.
8. Lippitt G. and Lippitt R. *THE CONSULTING PROCESS IN ACTION*, University Associates.
9. Association for Management Education and Development. For address see p.76.
10. Institute of Personnel Management, I. P. M. House, Camp Rd. Wimbledon SW19 4UW. Tel. 01-946 9100.
11. The Business Network, 18 Well Walk, Hampstead, London NW3 1LD. Tel. 01-435 5000.
12. Belbin R. M. *MANAGEMENT TEAMS: WHY THEY SUCCEED OR FAIL*, Heinemann 1981.
13. Handy C. *UNDERSTANDING ORGANIZATIONS*, Penguin 1976.

Appendix II A Checklist of Consultant Competences

Below we list some key areas of effectiveness for a consultant, divided under three main headings:

Personal and Interpersonal Effectiveness
Working as an agent of change
Consulting skills

The checklist is intended to guide personal reflection in identifying development needs. It can also be used for self- and peer-assessment.

Personal and interpersonal effectiveness

1. *Self-knowledge:* awareness of the values and beliefs that influence the way I work. Awareness of my own motivations and the personal rewards I derive from consulting. Awareness of the ethical choices I do, and would, make when faced with difficult, conflicting options.
2. *Self-awareness:* awareness of my own emotional response to situations and people, particularly awareness of patterns which may lead to inflexible behaviour.
3. *Active listening:* attending to the content and process level in

communication. Being attuned to non-verbal signals and their possible meaning. Ability to draw others out. Diagnosing possible underlying feelings, concerns and motivations.

4. *Self-expression:* ability to express my own thoughts, ideas and feelings clearly. Awareness of incongruities in my verbal and non-verbal expression.

5. *Relationship-building:* building open, collaborative relationships. Exchanging feedback in a timely and constructive way. Being assertive, when appropriate, particularly with authority figures. Balancing support and challenge in relationships. Ability to influence others and gain commitment. Being open to influence from others.

6. *Conflict-handling:* valuing and exploring differences. Ability to challenge without alienating. Maintaining flexibility, choice and self-esteem when faced with conflict and hostility. Having the personal courage to open up potentially difficult areas.

7. *Personal and professional limits*: awareness of the limits of my own competence. Willingness to ask for help. Willingness to admit my own mistakes without loss of self-confidence. Commitment to my on-going development.

Working as an agent of change

8. *Tolerance of ambiguity:* ability to live with uncertainty and complexity without undue stress. Searching for meaning without grasping at over-simplistic interpretations or rushing into premature action. Tolerating incompleteness.

9. *Maintaining a long-term perspective:* helping clients identify and articulate desired futures. Setting short- and medium-term goals in the light of a longer-term sense of purpose.

10. *Maintaining a wide perspective*: attending to the wider context of my work. Not drawing boundaries too tightly. Dealing with each subsystem's interaction with its suprasystem. Keeping abreast of trends and developments in organizational, business and world affairs.

11. *Understanding the nature of change:* developing an intellectual and experiential understanding of change processes – how and why people change, how and why they avoid change, how larger systems change or avoid changing.

12. *Facilitating change:* encouraging widespread participation in the design and implementation of change. Supporting others through the stress of transition. Being aware of myself as a catalyst and seeing the possibilities of intervention in all aspects of my work and interaction with clients.

Consulting skills

13. *Agreeing working contracts:* clarifying mutual expectations and responsibilities. Renegotiating the terms of my work when necessary.
14. *Data collection:* choosing appropriate methods of data collection. Asking pertinent questions. Formulating useful questions. Encouraging client ownership of data.
15. *Diagnosis:* having a range of frameworks and models for understanding individuals, groups and organizations. Maintaining a critical approach to models. Ability to construct my own models. Encouraging joint diagnosis with my clients.
16. *Design:* being creative and purposeful in designing interventions. Not relying on packaged, favourite interventions. Being willing to redesign on the spot. Designing at the level of content and process simultaneously.
17. *Closure:* disengaging well from assignments. Avoiding mutual dependency with my clients. Reviewing learning from each project.

Suggested Reading

The following list of books and articles is divided into four sections corresponding to the main themes of this book. These are:

The trends of change.
From training to consulting.
From training to learning.
From individual to organizational change.

We have already referred to some of the titles; others provide additional ideas in each area.

The trends of change

THE AQUARIAN CONSPIRACY, M. Ferguson (Paladin 1982). An attempt to synthesize the trends of change in all aspects of the humanites, politics, science, and religious and philosophical thought.
THE FUTURE OF WORK, C. Handy (Blackwell 1985). Looks at possibilities in changing work patterns, e.g. shorter careers, more part-time work and self-employment. Redefines 'work' and ways of organizing.
FUTURE WORK, J. Robertson (Temple Smith/Gower 1985). Covers similar areas as Handy's book, but is more radical.
MEGATRENDS, J. Naisbitt (Macdonald 1982). Describes ten trends of change which are restructuring American society.

THE ADAPTIVE CORPORATION, A. Toffler (Pan 1985). Uses a major study of AT&T (the American Telephone and Telegraph Company) to describe and comment on organizational response to changes in the environment.

REINVENTING THE CORPORATION, J. Naisbitt and P. Aburdene (Macdonald 1985). Describes some of the major social trends and their implications for managing organizations.

THE CHANGE MASTERS, R. M. Kanter (Counterpoint 1985). The result of research carried out in 'successful' and 'unsuccessful' organizations. A blend of theory and case-study material.

IN SEARCH OF EXCELLENCE, T. J. Peters and R. H. Waterman (Harper and Row 1982). The bestseller which spawned a number of 'excellence' books and which describes key factors for organizational success such as being close to the customer and entrepreneurship.

A PASSION FOR EXCELLENCE, T. Peters and N. Austin (Collins 1985). A sequel to the above with more detailed case-study material.

CREATING EXCELLENCE, C. R. Hickman and M. A. Silva (Unwin 1985). A simple, well written book on generating and sustaining change as a manager. A number of useful exercises and checklists.

INFORMATION AND ORGANIZATIONS, Max Boisot (Fontana 1987). Looks at the structure of information and information sharing and implications for communication strategies.

OF BOXES, BUBBLES AND EFFECTIVE MANAGEMENT, D. K. Hurst (Harvard Business Review May/June 1984). A case study of the turn-around of an ailing company. Highlights the full range of managerial competences needed to lead today's organizations.

From training to consulting

IMPROVING TRAINER EFFECTIVENESS, R. Bennett (ed.) (Gower 1988). A collection of papers reviewing the changing role of trainers.

'Tomorrow's Industrial Training Officer: The challenge of change', E. Donnelly, *JOURNAL OF EUROPEAN INDUS-TRIAL TRAINING*, Vol. 9, No. 5, 1985. Traces the historical development of the training role and suggests trends for the future.

'Pattern and Paradoxes of Trainers' Careers. The implications for the influence of training', J. Davies, *JOURNAL OF EURO-PEAN INDUSTRIAL TRAINING*, Vol. 9, No. 2, 1985. Research which identified different trainer roles and self-con-cepts and their consequences for trainers and organizations.

'Training for Change: A case-study of the Trainer's Role', M. Walton, *JOURNAL OF EUROPEAN INDUSTRIAL TRAINING*, Vol. 10, No. 4, 1986. Uses a case-study to illustrate the difference between Trainer/Consultant roles.

FLAWLESS CONSULTING: A GUIDE TO GETTING YOUR EXPERTISE USED P. Block (Learning Concepts 1981). An excellent, practical, well written book with useful guidelines and checklists.

CONSULTATION SKILLS READINGS, R. J. Lee and A. Freedman (eds) (N. T. L. Institute 1984). A collection of brief papers linked to the N. T. L. programmes for consultants.

CONSULTATION; A HANDBOOK FOR INDIVIDUAL AND ORGANIZATION DEVELOPMENT, R. Blake and J. S. Mouton (Addison-Wesley 1976). An exhaustive description of the range of consulting possibilities within the framework of the authors 'consulcube', which defines each consultation in terms of three parameters: size of client system, focal issues dealt with and type of intervention.

'Consulting is more than Giving Advice', A. N. Turner, *HAR-VARD BUSINESS REVIEW*, Sept/Oct 1982. Describes a hierarchy of consulting purposes.

From training to learning

MANAGEMENT SELF-DEVELOPMENT: CONCEPTS AND PRACTICES, T. Boydell and M. Pedler (eds) (Gower 1981). A valuable collection of readings including principles, designs and studies.

'Learning to Learn for Managers', A. Mumford, *JOURNAL*

OF EUROPEAN INDUSTRIAL TRAINING, Vol. 10, No. 2, 1986. A report which reviews the various approaches to 'learning to learn' and suggests the directions for further development.

IMPROVING WORK GROUPS; A PRACTICAL MANUAL FOR TEAM BUILDING, D. Francis and D. Young (University Associates 1979). Contains many useful suggestions, methods, questionnaires, activities etc.

'Developing within the Organization: Experiences of Management Self Development Groups', M. Pedler, *MEAD,* Vol. 17, Part 1, Spring 1986. Describes an MSC-funded project to research the outcomes and benefits of membership of self-development groups in a number of organizations.

'Promoting natural Learning Activities within the Organization', T. N, Garavan, *JOURNAL OF EUROPEAN INDUSTRIAL TRAINING,* Vol. 11, No.7, 1987. Describes development as the joint responsibility of managers and T and D specialists.

'Using Reality in Management Development', A. Mumford (*MEAD*, Vol. 18, Part 3, Autumn 1987). A call to use managers' everyday reality for 'live' management development.

'Management Learning Contracts: from theory to practice', G. Boak and M. Stephenson, *JOURNAL OF EUROPEAN INDUSTRIAL TRAINING,* Vol. 11, No. 4, 1987 and Vol. 11, No. 6, 1987. Describes the ingredients of a learning contract.

'How 'Self' Directed is Self Directed Learning?', G. Robertson, *MEAD*, Vol. 18, Part 2, Summer 1987. A challenging review of the values and assumptions behind self-development.

THE LEARNING ORGANIZATION, B. Garratt (Fontana Gower 1987). A guide to the development of directors to promote their own learning and that of the companies they lead.

From individual to organizational change

CHANGE; PRINCIPLES OF PROBLEM FORMATION AND PROBLEM RESOLUTION, P. Watzlawick, J. Weakland and R. Fisch (Norton 1974). A seminal work which has influenced current thinking in training therapy and consulting.

STRATEGIES FOR MANAGING CHANGE, W. G. Dyer (Addison-Wesley 1984). A straightforward guide to planned change with a useful matrix of possible interventions.

'MANAGING THE HUMAN SIDE OF CHANGE', R. Moss Kanter, *Management Review*, April 1985. Contains a useful analysis of the reasons managers resist change.

VISUALIZING CHANGE: MODEL BUILDING AND THE CHANGE PROCESS, G. Lippitt (University Associates 1973). A rigorous classification and description of change models; how to use them and construct them.

IMAGES OF ORGANIZATIONS, G. Morgan (Sage 1986). An inspiring book which describes different ways of conceptualizing about organizations.

ORGANIZATIONAL CULTURE AND LEADERSHIP, E. Schein (Jossey Bass 1985). An elegant and comprehensive blend of theory and research.

SYSTEMS BEHAVIOUR, Open Systems Group (ed.) (Harper and Row 1985). An Open University set book on open systems theory and its applications.

THE NEUROTIC ORGANIZATION, M. Kets de Vries and D. Miller (Jossey Bass 1985). A review of organizational problems by analogy with individual psychological disorders.

THE NEUROTIC BEHAVIOUR OF ORGANIZATIONS, V. Merry and G. I. Brown (Gestalt Institute of Cleveland Press 1987). Takes ideas from Gestalt psychotherapy and applies them to organizational consulting.

EVERYBODY WINS: TRANSACTIONAL ANALYSIS APPLIED TO ORGANIZATIONS, D. Jongeward and contributors (Addison-Wesley 1978). The title is self-explanatory.

Four titles are classic OD texts.

ORGANIZATION DEVELOPMENT: ITS NATURE, ORIGINS AND PROSPECTS, W. G. Bennis (Addison-Wesley 1969).

DEVELOPING ORGANIZATIONS; DIAGNOSIS AND ACTION, P. R. Lawrence and J. W. Lorsch (Addison-Wesley 1969).

ORGANIZATION DEVELOPMENT: STRATEGIES AND MODELS, R. Beckhard (Addison-Wesley 1969).

PROCESS CONSULTATION : ITS ROLE IN ORGANIZA-

TION DEVELOPMENT, E. Schein (Addison-Wesley 1969).
CAREER DYNAMICS : MATCHING INDIVIDUAL AND ORGANIZATIONAL NEEDS, E. Schein (Addison-Wesley 1978). Describes the organizational implications of life and career changes.
MANAGING WITH PEOPLE: A MANAGER'S HANDBOOK, J. K. Fordyce and R. Weil (Addison-Wesley 1983). A good overview of OD methods, emphasizing collaboration between managers and OD specialists.

Two collections of theory and practice in organizational intervention.

NEW TECHNOLOGIES IN ORGANIZATION DEVELOPMENT 1, W. W. Burke (ed.) (University Associates 1975).
NEW TECHNOLOGIES IN ORGANIZATION DEVELOPMENT 2, J. D. Adams (ed.) (University Associates 1975).

These two collections of readings come from the emerging school of organizational transformation practitioners, who take a more holistic and spiritual approach to organization change consulting.

TRANSFORMING WORK, J. Adams (ed.) (Miles River Press 1984).
TRANSFORMING LEADERSHIP, J. Adams (ed.) (Miles River Press 1986).

Index

action learning sets, 4, 9, 79, 148–9
Adams, John, 6
ambiguity
  in consultancy, 23
  in relationships, 35–6
  tolerance of, 5, 107, 154
applause, 28, 29–30, 31, 32
assignments *see under* learning:
  consultant; organization
  change: consultant; training:
  consultant
Association for Management
  Education and Development
  (AMED), 63, 149
audience, performing to, 28, 29–32
Austin, N., 63

Beckhard, Richard, 103–4
Belbin, R. M., 111–12
Bennett, Ben, 118
Block, Peter, 33, 38
Bolton-Smith Ltd, 125–40
boundaries, 112
brainstorming, 148
British Airways, 2–3
British Rail, 2–3
Business Network, The, 149

cellular structures, 3
certainty, 34–6

challenge, constructive, 50–51
change
  continuous, 2, 86–7, 103
  organizational, 1–11, 100–123
  paradigm shifts, 141–4
  understanding, 154, 155
charts, organization, 109–10
clients
  definition of, 38, 54–5
  relationship with consultants, 22,
    35–6, 43, 44–51, 58–9, 73
closure, 155
co-counselling, 148
collaboration *see* relationships
competence
  basis for, 142–3
  for consultancy, 40–2, 153–5
  emotional, 5
  see also experience of trainers
conflict-handling, 87, 154
consultants and consultancy
  definition of 38
  see also development; experience
    of trainers; external; internal;
    learning; organization change;
    organizational development;
    training: consultants
consulting cycle model, 22, 39–40
continuous change, 2, 86–7, 103
contracts

163